I0409899

# U.S. FOREIGN POLICY TOWARD UKRAINE

# HEARING

BEFORE THE

## COMMITTEE ON FOREIGN AFFAIRS
## HOUSE OF REPRESENTATIVES

ONE HUNDRED THIRTEENTH CONGRESS

SECOND SESSION

MARCH 6, 2014

**Serial No. 113–129**

Printed for the use of the Committee on Foreign Affairs

Available via the World Wide Web: http://www.foreignaffairs.house.gov/ or
http://www.gpo.gov/fdsys/

U.S. GOVERNMENT PRINTING OFFICE

86–960PDF                    WASHINGTON : 2014

For sale by the Superintendent of Documents, U.S. Government Printing Office
Internet: bookstore.gpo.gov   Phone: toll free (866) 512–1800; DC area (202) 512–1800
Fax: (202) 512–2104   Mail: Stop IDCC, Washington, DC 20402–0001

## COMMITTEE ON FOREIGN AFFAIRS

EDWARD R. ROYCE, California, *Chairman*

CHRISTOPHER H. SMITH, New Jersey
ILEANA ROS-LEHTINEN, Florida
DANA ROHRABACHER, California
STEVE CHABOT, Ohio
JOE WILSON, South Carolina
MICHAEL T. McCAUL, Texas
TED POE, Texas
MATT SALMON, Arizona
TOM MARINO, Pennsylvania
JEFF DUNCAN, South Carolina
ADAM KINZINGER, Illinois
MO BROOKS, Alabama
TOM COTTON, Arkansas
PAUL COOK, California
GEORGE HOLDING, North Carolina
RANDY K. WEBER SR., Texas
SCOTT PERRY, Pennsylvania
STEVE STOCKMAN, Texas
RON DeSANTIS, Florida
DOUG COLLINS, Georgia
MARK MEADOWS, North Carolina
TED S. YOHO, Florida
LUKE MESSER, Indiana

ELIOT L. ENGEL, New York
ENI F.H. FALEOMAVAEGA, American Samoa
BRAD SHERMAN, California
GREGORY W. MEEKS, New York
ALBIO SIRES, New Jersey
GERALD E. CONNOLLY, Virginia
THEODORE E. DEUTCH, Florida
BRIAN HIGGINS, New York
KAREN BASS, California
WILLIAM KEATING, Massachusetts
DAVID CICILLINE, Rhode Island
ALAN GRAYSON, Florida
JUAN VARGAS, California
BRADLEY S. SCHNEIDER, Illinois
JOSEPH P. KENNEDY III, Massachusetts
AMI BERA, California
ALAN S. LOWENTHAL, California
GRACE MENG, New York
LOIS FRANKEL, Florida
TULSI GABBARD, Hawaii
JOAQUIN CASTRO, Texas

AMY PORTER, *Chief of Staff*     THOMAS SHEEHY, *Staff Director*
JASON STEINBAUM, *Democratic Staff Director*

(II)

# CONTENTS

# U.S. FOREIGN POLICY TOWARD UKRAINE

---

## THURSDAY, MARCH 6, 2014

House of Representatives,
Committee on Foreign Affairs,
*Washington, DC.*

The committee met, pursuant to notice, at 9:05 a.m., in room 2172 Rayburn House Office Building, Hon. Edward Royce (chairman of the committee) presiding.

Chairman ROYCE. I am going to call the hearing to order at this time. We will ask all the members if they can come in and take their seats for this hearing.

Let me begin by pointing out that Ukraine is facing not one crisis but a number of them. Its new government is confronting an economic and financial crisis brought on by years of mismanagement, years of corruption by previous government officials and it is doing this while under military invasion and economic coercion by neighboring Russia. The world has been speaking up, sending a clear message and that message is that Moscow's actions over the past week are out of bounds.

The new government in Kiev cannot succeed without strong and rapid support by the international community. Working in close cooperation with our European allies, the U.S. is crafting an immediate assistance package. But this help must be accompanied by fundamental economic reforms if Ukraine is to stabilize its economy. Only Ukraine can help us help them.

I will also mention that later this month, prior to the elections in Ukraine, I will be leading a codel to the country because we must also help to ensure that the elections scheduled for May will be fair, will be free and reflect the true voice of the Ukrainian people in all regions of the country, a country that is becoming increasingly divided, and I think our oversight and engagement there right now is very important. A successful election is essential to Ukraine's ability to resolve the many issues its got on its plate and to advance toward democracy and security, and long-term toward prosperity.

Addressing Ukraine's energy security must be part of our response. Russia has repeatedly used its supply of natural gas to pressure Ukraine economically and politically, and has announced that it will significantly increase its cost in a deliberate effort to squeeze Ukraine.

Fortunately, we have an option to help counter this threat, namely, reducing the current impediments to exports of American gas to the Ukraine. The administration has it within its power to

2

do this by removing the current bureaucratic obstacles that only empower Putin. They should do so rapidly.

This committee is working to provide appropriate assistance to all Ukrainian people but also to pressure Russia to withdraw its forces and cease its efforts to destabilize Ukraine. As part of that effort, immediately following this hearing, we will mark up a resolution that the ranking member and I have introduced that condemns Russia's aggression and outlines these steps.

I strongly encourage the administration to increase efforts to isolate Russia diplomatically. There is much that should be done, such as introducing a resolution at the U.N. Security Council that condemns Russian aggression, isolating Moscow.

The rest of the international community will support such a resolution. Moscow alone will veto it but it will increase the pressure.

The Treasury Department should also make clear that the U.S. is on the lookout for Russian banks that are involved in illicit activities, such as the transfer of stolen Ukrainian assets, and especially those banks that are primarily owned by the government or by the oligarchs. We also in our resolution lay out other steps that should be taken such as the limitation on travel.

Many of us have been calling for action and last evening the administration called me to indicate that it was going to take steps on precisely these issues—the visa and asset bans here—and so we will look forward to that statement from the administration I think further elaborating on the Executive order announced early this morning.

But we must remember that the purpose of our pressure on Russia is not simply to punish aggression and certainly it is not to escalate the confrontation, but instead to move Putin toward a resolution that protects the territorial integrity of Ukraine.

That is our ambition here, and as we look forward we have with us today three administration witnesses to answer questions from members regarding the current situation in Ukraine and the administration's ongoing efforts to provide assistance to Kiev and to pressure Russia.

The ranking member will be here shortly and while he is en route I will also take this opportunity to introduce our witnesses. We have limited time this morning so before I introduce the witnesses we are honored to have with us today Ambassador Motsyk from the Embassy of Ukraine.

Mr. Ambassador, we know that it is a very difficult time for your country and we want to extend a very warm welcome to you. As you can see, Ukraine has many friends on this committee.

This morning we are pleased to be joined by representatives from the Department of State, the U.S. Agency for International Development, and the Department of the Treasury.

A career Foreign Service officer, Mr. Eric Rubin previously served as Deputy Chief of Mission at the U.S. Embassy in Moscow from 2008 until 2011 before assuming his duties as Deputy Assistant Secretary in the Bureau of European and Eurasian Affairs.

With over 20 years of experience working in international development in the region, Ms. Paige Alexander is the Assistant Administrator of the Bureau for Europe and Eurasia at the U.S. Agency for International Development.

Mr. Daleep Singh is the Deputy Assistant Secretary for Europe and Eurasia at the U.S. Department of the Treasury. He advises the senior economic leadership at the Department of Treasury and the White House on global markets.

And without objection, the witnesses' full prepared statements are going to be made part of the record. I am going to encourage you all to summarize and just use your time to present your viewpoints and afterwards the members will have 5 calendar days to submit statements and questions and any extraneous materials for the record.

Without objection, as member offices were notified last night, in light of our time constraint Mr. Engel and I are suggesting we limit to 3 minutes per member to help maximize participation of all the members this morning.

And if I could now go to our ranking member, Mr. Engel, whose family is originally from the Ukraine—Mr. Eliot Engel from New York.

Mr. ENGEL. Thank you. Thank you very much, Mr. Chairman.

Deputy Assistant Rubin, Assistant Administrator Alexander, Deputy Assistant Secretary Singh, thank you for appearing before the committee today and for your tireless efforts over the past several months in support of Ukraine.

And let me thank Chairman Royce for calling this hearing on an issue which is at the forefront of all our minds right now.

Since 1991, the U.S. has strongly supported a democratic, prosperous, sovereign Ukraine, and in keeping with this commitment we supported a peaceful negotiated resolution of the recent crisis there, as hundreds of thousands of Ukrainian citizens came out in the streets of Kiev and throughout Ukraine to express their desire for a more democratic and just state.

The recent selection of a new interim government signaled that Ukraine was back on the path toward stability and political and economic health. But instead of welcoming this event, as was the case in the U.S. and Europe, President Putin has reacted in a very different and very disturbing manner.

So let me be clear. President Putin's aggressive military actions in Crimea flagrantly violate Ukraine's sovereignty and territorial integrity. They violate international law and they violate Russia's commitments to Ukraine.

They are deeply destabilizing and have serious implications for security in Europe. All of us should be profoundly concerned about this.

And furthermore, his justification for this aggression is completely unsupported by the facts. There has been no persecution of Russians or Russian speakers in Ukraine. All credible observers agree on this point.

So I believe this is a critical moment. The U.S., our European allies and the international community must stand up for Ukraine's unity and territorial integrity. Russia has deep historical and cultural ties with Ukraine and Russia and Ukraine should enjoy good and close relations.

President Putin must respect Ukraine's sovereignty and the right of its people to freely make their own choices and chart their own future and Russia must also understand that there are consequences for its aggression.

I think we should consider a range of sanctions including visa bans, freezing assets, and banking sanctions so that President Putin understands that this will not be business as usual.

I call on our European allies and other members of the international community to take similar measures. I also support the administration's initiative to send international observers to monitor the situation in Crimea and other parts of Ukraine.

Russia, in turn, should welcome such a mission, return its troops to their bases immediately and comply with its commitments. Our other immediate priority should be to help Ukraine's interim government deal with the formidable challenges that it faces. Secretary Kerry was just in Kiev, and this was the right time to go and the right way to show our support.

Given Ukraine's dire economic situation, we and our European allies should be ready to provide a robust assistance pledge. I strongly support the administration's initiative to provide loan guarantees to Ukraine and I am very pleased that the House will pass legislation authorizing these guarantees later today.

I also welcome the EU's announcement that it also will provide very sufficient loans and credits and, of course, we must also support Ukraine's efforts to reach an agreement with the IMF and implement reforms to address structural weaknesses.

We should also provide additional assistance in areas of urgent need, such as to help Ukraine recover looted assets, combat corruption, conduct free and fair new elections, increase energy security and counter politically motivated trade actions by Russia.

With regard to this last point, I also believe we and the EU must steadfastly support other nations facing similar Russian pressure, such as Moldova and Georgia. As Ukraine's leaders restore stability and order in the country, I urge them to reach out to all groups and regions and to work together to build a tolerant, pluralistic society.

The interim government and any Ukrainian Government must protect the rights of all minority populations and make it clear that it represents all Ukrainian citizens.

Let me take this opportunity to say a word about anti-Semitism, which has been mentioned as another justification for Russian military aggression.

I recognize that there is a concern, but as the respected NCSJ recently stated, and I quote,

> "While there has been isolated incidents in Crimea and eastern Ukraine since the protests began in November, there has not been a pattern of violence against the Ukrainian Jewish population."

And finally, let me once more thank our witnesses and the administration for its tireless efforts over the past several months to support democracy in Ukraine. As the people of Ukraine confront the many challenges ahead, they should know that the United States will stand with them.

We will support Ukraine's sovereignty and territorial integrity and we will support Ukrainian aspirations to build a more democratic, prosperous and just future for their country.

Thank you, Mr. Chairman.

Chairman ROYCE. Thank you. We are going to go to Mr. Rubin.

## STATEMENT OF MR. ERIC RUBIN, DEPUTY ASSISTANT SECRETARY, BUREAU OF EUROPEAN AND EURASIAN AFFAIRS, U.S. DEPARTMENT OF STATE

Mr. RUBIN. Thank you, Chairman Royce, Ranking Member Engel, members of this committee. I am grateful for the opportunity to speak to you today on U.S. policy toward Ukraine.

I would also like to express appreciation for Ukrainian Ambassador Motsyk joining us today. We very much appreciate his presence. Let me begin by thanking this committee for its deep engagement on this issue.

In our efforts to back the aspirations of the Ukrainian people, we have been heartened by the robust bipartisan support that we have received from this committee and from Congress more broadly.

House Resolution 447, introduced by Ranking Member Engel and passed by the House on February 10th, sent a powerful message that the American people stand wholly and unequivocally with the people of Ukraine in their hour of need. You have notified us that you are marking up a new resolution today and we welcome your leadership.

We have had close and constant contact with Congress in every step of this grave situation. Our united efforts have demonstrated to the people of Ukraine and to the international community that the United States is resolute in its support of Ukraine's desire for a democratic, peaceful and prosperous future.

I would like to address two areas in my remarks. I will begin by discussing the political situation in Ukraine. Second, I will talk about regional stability, Russia's military intervention in Ukraine and the response of the United States and the international community to Russia's action.

I have submitted a more detailed written testimony for the record. I underscore that the situation in the region is extremely fluid and changing by the hour. We continue to adapt as it evolves.

I would also like to underscore that the situation has changed as recently as this morning and we have taken additional actions as recently as this morning, which I am prepared to discuss in further detail.

Let me also add a few words about my own deep personal commitment to Ukraine and its future. I first worked to support the Ukrainian people and their aspirations for freedom in 1989 when I was the internal politics and nationalities affairs officer on the Soviet desk of the State Department.

I helped open relations with independent Ukraine in 1991, and my wife and I lived and worked in Kiev from 1994 to 1996 in the early days of Ukraine's independence.

I speak Ukrainian and I have friends throughout Ukraine. Over the tumultuous events of the past several months, I have watched with horror as Ukrainians were cut down by snipers in the heart of Kiev.

But I have also been inspired by the people of Ukraine—their determination, their courage, and their insistence on the possibility of a better future for themselves and their country.

I would like to start by emphasizing that the democratic transition that has occurred in Ukraine is an expression of will of the Ukrainian people. It is not about the United States. It is not about Russia.

The people of Ukraine have made a decision about their future. The Rada, the country's democratically-elected Parliament, has taken the steps of creating a transitional government following former President Yanukovych's abdication.

Ukraine's lawmakers in the Rada have fulfilled their obligation to the people by preparing to tackle pressing economic and political issues facing the country until new Presidential elections can be held in May.

These decisions have been supported by overwhelming majorities in the Rada including members of President Yanukovych's party. The United States welcomed the formation of the new government and is working with its leadership as it ensures the protection of the rights of all Ukrainians including all minorities.

As the international community looks for ways to help Ukraine, we will focus on the government's efforts to build a strong, sovereign and democratic country reflecting the will of the people of Ukraine.

The decision of the Ukrainian people regarding their government needs to be respected. Russia's military intervention in Ukraine has endangered the promise of Ukraine's democratic transition.

As Secretary Kerry said in Kiev on Tuesday,

> "The contrast could not be clearer—determined Ukrainians demonstrating strength through unity and a Russian Government out of excuses, hiding its hand behind falsehoods, intimidation and provocations."

The United States fully and unambiguously condemns Russia's military intervention in Ukrainian territory. We have repeatedly indicated that Russia's actions in Crimea are a violation of Ukrainian sovereignty and territorial integrity and a breach of international law, including Russia's obligations under the U.N. Charter and of its 1997 Treaty of Friendship with Ukraine as well as Russia's basing agreement of 1997 with Ukraine.

Russia agreed in that treaty to respect the sovereignty of Ukraine and not to interfere in Ukraine's internal affairs. This is also a blatant affront to the 1994 Budapest Memorandum and the Helsinki Final Act.

We have already taken actions consistent with the unacceptability of Russia's military intervention. Shoulder to shoulder with our G–7 counterparts, we have suspended participation in the G–8 Sochi preparations.

We have suspended all talks with Russia on any future trade or investment agreements. We have suspended military to military contacts. We have issued a statement with the unanimous approval of the members of the North Atlantic Council strongly condemning the Russian military escalation in Crimea.

NATO is stepping up efforts to increase our Baltic air policing mission and we are working on ways to strengthen our aviation detachment cooperation with Poland.

We are considering other measures to provide reassurance to our allies, and today the United States has marshalled a full package of measures aimed at demonstrating the force of U.S. resolve in the face of unprovoked military aggression, intervention and threats.

Pursuant to the President's guidance, the State Department is putting in place visa restrictions on a number of officials and individuals, reflecting a policy decision to deny visas to those responsible for or complicit in threatening the sovereignty and territorial integrity of Ukraine.

In addition, the President has signed an Executive order that authorizes sanctions on individuals and entities responsible for activities undermining democratic processes or institutions in Ukraine, threatening the peace, security, stability, sovereignty or territorial integrity of Ukraine, contributing to the misappropriation of state assets of Ukraine, or purporting to assert governmental authority over any part of Ukraine without authorization from the Ukrainian Government in Kiev.

We have made it clear to Russia and others that steps to undermine Ukrainian democracy and territorial integrity will result in further political and economic isolation should they continue on this path.

Mr. Chairman, our focus remains on de-escalation of tensions. We continue to explore the possibility of an ''off-ramp'' that could lead to the relaxation of tensions in Ukraine, if the Russians are willing to take it.

We support direct talks between the Ukrainian and Russian Governments. Secretary Kerry met yesterday in Paris separately with the foreign ministers of Ukraine and Russia as well as with European counterparts in an effort to get such talks going.

The OSCE and the United Nations are in the process of deploying monitors in the country, including Crimea and eastern Ukraine. These monitors will provide transparency about the activity of military and para-military forces, monitors for abuse and defuse tensions between groups.

They, along with senior delegations from our NATO allies to the region, will offer objective on-the-ground information to counteract Russia's flagrant propaganda campaign.

And let me be clear on this point. There are no confirmed reports of threats to ethnic Russians. No confirmed reports of a massive movement of ethnic Russian refugees. No threat to Russian naval bases.

The interim Ukrainian Government is a body that represents the will of the Ukrainian people. It is not an extremist cabal. Russia's assertions are nothing more than a veneer used to justify its military action.

I would also like to state before this committee that the United States is closely monitoring reports of anti-Semitic acts.

We take this issue very, very seriously. It is an issue I have worked on for more than 20 years personally and I would like to concur with the statement that you made indicating that we have no such information indicating that there are widespread anti-Semitic incidents.

We have been in touch with the chief rabbi, with leaders of all the major Jewish groups in Ukraine and we believe that this accusation is, again, being used to justify an unjustifiable military intervention.

[The prepared statement of Mr. Rubin follows:]

**Eric Rubin**
**Deputy Assistant Secretary of State for European and Eurasian Affairs**
**House Committee on Foreign Affairs**
**March 6, 2014 U.S. Foreign Policy Toward Ukraine**

Chairman Royce, Ranking Member Engel, members of this Committee, I am grateful for the opportunity to speak to you today on U.S. foreign policy toward Ukraine.

Let me begin by thanking this Committee for its deep engagement on this issue. In our efforts to back the aspirations of the Ukrainian people, we have been heartened by the robust bipartisan support that we have received from this Committee and from Congress more broadly. House Resolution 447 introduced by Ranking Member Engel and passed by the House on February 10, sent a powerful message that the American people stand wholly and unequivocally with the people of Ukraine in their hour of need.

We have had close and constant contact with Congress in every step of this grave situation. Our united efforts have demonstrated to the people of Ukraine and to the international community that the United States is resolute in its support of Ukraine's desire for a democratic, peaceful, and prosperous future.

I would like to address four areas in my remarks. I will begin by discussing the political situation in Ukraine. Second, I will talk about regional stability, Russia's military intervention in Ukraine and the response of the United States and the international community to Russia's action. Third, I will briefly touch on Ukraine's current perilous economic situation and the tools necessary in the immediate and mid-term to begin the process of economic healing after years of severe mismanagement. My colleague from Treasury will build on this more thoroughly. Finally, I will briefly address U.S. technical assistance in Ukraine and support for the country's return to the normal democratic process.

I underscore that the situation in the region is extremely fluid. We continue to adapt as it rapidly evolves.

Let me also add a few words about my own deep personal commitment to Ukraine and its future. I first worked to support the Ukrainian people and their aspirations for freedom in 1989, when I was the internal politics and nationalities affairs officer on the Soviet Desk at the State Department. I helped open relations with independent Ukraine in 1991, and my wife and I lived in Kyiv from 1994 through 1996, in the early days of Ukraine's independence. I speak Ukrainian, and I have friends throughout Ukraine. Over the tumultuous events of the past several months, I have watched with horror as Ukrainians were cut down by snipers in the heart of Kyiv. But I have also been inspired by the people of Ukraine—their determination, their courage, and their insistence on the possibility of a better future for themselves and their country.

**Political Situation**
I would like to start by emphasizing that the democratic transition that occurred in Ukraine was an expression of will of the Ukrainian people. This is not about the United States. This is not about Russia.

The people of Ukraine have made a decision about their future. The Rada, the country's democratically elected legislature, has taken the step of creating a transitional government following former president Yanukovych's abdication. Ukraine's lawmakers in the Rada have fulfilled their obligation to the people by preparing to tackle the pressing economic and political issues facing the country until new presidential elections can be held in May. These decisions have been supported by overwhelming majorities in the Rada including members of Yanukovych's former party.

The United States welcomed the formation of the new government and is working with its leadership as it ensures the protection of the rights of all Ukrainians including all minorities. As the international community looks for ways to help Ukraine, we will focus on the government's efforts to build the strong, sovereign and democratic country the people of Ukraine desire and so richly deserve. The decision of the Ukrainian people regarding their government needs to be respected.

**Implications for stability in the region**
Russia's military intervention in Ukraine, however, has endangered the promise of Ukraine's democratic transition. As Secretary Kerry said in Kyiv on Tuesday, "the contrast could not be clearer: determined Ukrainians demonstrating strength through unity and a Russian Government out of excuses, hiding its hand behind falsehoods, intimidation, and provocations."

The United States fully and unambiguously condemns Russia's military intervention in Ukrainian territory. We have repeatedly indicated that Russia's actions in Crimea are in clear violation of Ukrainian sovereignty and territorial integrity and a breach of international law, including Russia's obligations under the UN Charter, and of its 1997 Treaty of Friendship, Cooperation, and Partnership and of its military basing agreement with Ukraine in which it agreed to respect the sovereignty of Ukraine and not to interfere in Ukraine's internal affairs. It is also a blatant affront to the 1994 Budapest Memorandum and the Helsinki Final Act.

We have already taken actions consistent with the unacceptability of Russia's military intervention. Shoulder to shoulder with our G7 counterparts, we have suspended participation in the G8 Sochi preparations. We have suspended all talks with Russia on any future trade or investment agreements. We have suspended military to military contacts. We issued a statement with the unanimous approval of the members of the North Atlantic Council strongly condemning the Russian military escalation in Crimea. NATO is stepping up efforts to increase the Baltic air policing mission. We are working on ways to strengthen our aviation detachment cooperation with Poland. We are considering other measures to provide reassurance to our allies.

And today the United States has marshalled a full package of measures aimed at demonstrating the force of U.S. resolve in the face of unprovoked military intervention and threats. Pursuant to the President's guidance, the State Department is putting in place visa restrictions on a number of officials and individuals, reflecting a policy decision to deny visas to those responsible for or complicit in threatening the sovereignty and territorial integrity of Ukraine. In addition, the President has signed an Executive Order that authorizes sanctions on individuals and entities responsible for activities undermining democratic processes or institutions in Ukraine; threatening the peace, security, stability, sovereignty, or territorial integrity of Ukraine;

contributing to the misappropriation of state assets of Ukraine; or purporting to assert governmental authority over any part of Ukraine without authorization from the Ukrainian government in Kyiv. We have made it clear to Russia and others that steps to undermine Ukrainian democracy and territorial integrity will result in further political and economic isolation should they continue on this path.

Despite Russian obstinacy and deception, our focus remains on de-escalation of tensions. We continue to explore the possibility of an "off-ramp" that could lead to the relaxation of tensions in Ukraine, if the Russians are willing to take it. We support direct talks between the Ukrainian and Russian governments. Secretary Kerry met yesterday in Paris separately with the Foreign Ministers of Ukraine and Russia, as well as with European counterparts, in an effort to get such talks going. The OSCE and UN are in the process of deploying monitors in the country, including Crimea and Eastern Ukraine. These monitors will provide transparency about the activity of military and para-military forces, monitor for abuse, and defuse tensions between groups. They, along with senior delegations from NATO allies to the region, will offer objective on-the-ground information to counteract Russia's flagrant propaganda campaign.

And let me be clear on this point. There are no confirmed reports of threats to ethnic Russians. No confirmed reports of a massive movement of ethnic Russian refugees. No threat to Russian naval bases. The interim Ukrainian government is a body that represents the will of the people. It is not an extremist cabal. Russia's assertions are nothing more than a baseless veneer used to justify its military action.

I would also like to state before this committee that the United States is monitoring the reports of anti-Semitic acts extremely closely. We know that some organizations have expressed concern about the treatment of the Jewish community in Ukraine. We continue to emphasize to the leadership of all Ukrainian parties that there is no place for anti-Semitism in Ukraine's future.

With regard to relations with Russia, we will continue to work with Russia in areas in which we have a responsibility to the global community such as Syria and Iran. That said, we must speak frankly about Russia's action in Ukraine. While Russia is not an adversary, its actions in Ukraine are deeply adversarial – both to the rules of the international order and to the hopes and aspirations of the Ukrainian people.

**Economic Situation**
At the same time, Ukraine's financial situation remains deeply precarious. The political upheaval of recent months has added to long-term economic and fiscal problems rooted in systemic corruption and mismanagement that have choked the country's economic potential for years. Unsustainable economic policies under previous Ukrainian administrations have left Ukraine's economy uncompetitive and have eroded Ukraine's foreign reserves. Ukraine urgently needs to pursue economic reforms and secure external financing to restore economic stability .

In the immediate term, an International Monetary Fund (IMF) package provides the best foundation for economic advice and financing. Interim Prime Minister Yatsenyuk has stated that Ukraine needs to meet IMF conditions. Meeting these conditions will be tough. They will likely require reducing energy subsidies, a more flexible exchange rate, and reducing the budget deficit.

We welcome the new government's commitment to pursue reforms that could be supported by an IMF program. Additional multilateral and bilateral support for a reform program could help to ensure that Ukraine has the support it needs in order for reforms to be successful and give it space to take reform steps incrementally. Just yesterday the European Union announced that it would be providing $3 billion in bilateral financial support, which would be complemented by assistance from the EIB and the multilateral development banks, much of it linked to an IMF program.

And the United States stands ready to act as well. We are working with this Committee and others in Congress to provide a sovereign loan guarantee for Ukraine to help provide needed financing to the government at a key point in Ukraine's history in conjunction with an IMF program. This loan guarantee is an effective way to leverage U.S. assistance to Ukraine and achieve both political and economic foreign policy objectives. The Administration is also working with Congress to approve IMF quota legislation, which would support the IMF's capacity to lend additional resources to Ukraine and help preserve continued U.S. leadership within this important institution. Passing this legislation is vital national security priority.

The United States is committed to supporting reform efforts aimed at bolstering Ukraine in its economic recovery. Only the IMF can provide the amount of funding necessary to cover Ukraine's immediate and medium-term financing needs and restore economic stability. A loan guarantee from the United States could serve as an important complement to an IMF program by helping the government as it undertakes the required reforms. This loan guarantee will be the centerpiece of our bilateral assistance to help in this effort. We thank the Committee for its leadership and assistance in ensuring we can respond quickly to Ukraine's urgent financial needs.

Ukraine is only the latest example of how we rely on the IMF to be the first responder in economic crises. This is why we are consulting with Congress to approve IMF quota legislation, which help preserve continued U.S. leadership within this important institution. This reform would also support the IMF's capacity to lend additional resources to Ukraine. Passing this legislation is vital national security priority.

**Technical assistance**
In addition to financial assistance, the United States continues to deploy technical assistance tools as Ukraine struggles to get back on its political and economic feet. Since the political crisis began, we have been working within existing resources—both the existing bilateral budget for Ukraine and global funding sources--to be as responsive as possible to urgent needs.

So far, this has included a full range of important actions. Our first priority is to support the Ukrainian government as it prepares for elections in less than three months, including by ensuring that the elections environment is conducive to a free, fair and inclusive election. We have intensified our legal assistance project to assist journalists and activists. We have increased support to local civil society and independent media organizations. We have launched a cybersecurity project aimed at protecting local NGOs, activists, and media. We are providing objective information about European integration and rapidly unfolding current events in

Russian, with a particular emphasis in southern and eastern Ukraine. And we are assisting local journalists in developing local on-the-ground content.

We are reviewing our current resources to develop a package of additional assistance to the government of Ukraine in the near term and are working closely with USAID. We will consult with Congress as we put together a package which will prioritize programs to promote economic reform; conduct free and fair elections, battle corruption, strengthen the justice sector, and assist with asset recovery from corrupt officials; and help Ukraine weather trade and energy disruptions. Our assistance will also promote free, fair, and transparent elections on May 25.

**Conclusion**
As President Obama stated earlier this week, our national interest is in "seeing the Ukrainian people be able to determine their own destiny." The United States and our allies are committed to helping Ukraine realize the full potential of this moment. Russia has a choice to make. It can come to the table and support the Ukrainians as they chart their future. Or it can continue its current course of action and risk being frozen out.

Thank you again for inviting me to appear today, and for your focus on this critical set of issues. I look forward to your questions.

Chairman ROYCE. Thank you very much, Mr. Rubin.

Now, we have 5 minutes for opening statements and so, Paige, if you could summarize I think that is for the best.

Ms. Alexander.

## STATEMENT OF THE HONORABLE PAIGE ALEXANDER, ASSISTANT ADMINISTRATOR, BUREAU FOR EUROPE AND EURASIA, U.S. AGENCY FOR INTERNATIONAL DEVELOPMENT

Ms. ALEXANDER. Thank you. Thank you for inviting me here today regarding the U.S. assistance package for Ukraine.

Chairman ROYCE. Paige, go ahead and put the microphone there.

Ms. ALEXANDER. Sorry. Sorry. So recent events are momentous for Ukraine and the response of the United States Government is critical to the region's future.

The U.S. is working with our international partners, especially the International Monetary Fund, to provide needed support to Ukraine's people and the economy as they face this current crisis.

Our approach is to support the goals and aspirations of all people of Ukraine for peace, prosperity, freedom and human dignity—the very things that the people have been on the Maidan for the last 3 months explaining their concerns.

So as the chairman mentioned, for the upcoming elections USAID and our partners are moving forward with a series of programs in five specific areas to help ensure these elections are free, fair, transparent and inclusive.

We will work to improve the legal framework to strengthen election administration, support civic oversight of the electoral process through observation missions by domestic and international monitors, encourage civil society coalitions to advocate for further reforms, promote a more balanced, open and diverse information environment throughout the country and support a robust yet a fair political competition in informing the public through support for public opinion polls and ensuring training for party poll watchers.

We also recognize that the more inclusive and accountable governments will not be established with just one Presidential election.

Over the mid- to longer-term range, we will pursue a multifaceted approach to strengthening Ukraine's democratic institutions and process. Years of economic mismanagement have left Ukraine with a heavy debt burden, weak regulatory oversight of financial institutions and an uncompetitive business climate.

The ongoing economic instability has led to a heightened uncertainty in the financial sector, prompting the National Bank of Ukraine to impose capital controls as depositors become wary of the soundness of domestic banks.

Recognizing the serious potential for failed banks, USAID will work to help provide banking supervision to increase public confidence.

We realize that Ukraine's inefficient and import-dependent energy sector continues to be a significant drain on Ukraine's financial resources and this needs to be addressed in the medium term as well.

So U.S. technical assistance will be provided to the Government of Ukraine as it makes important policy reforms and combats the widespread corruption that has prevented Ukraine from reaching its economic potential.

We need to revitalize the support for the private sector which has staggered in recent years under an increasing and uneven playing field and official harassment.

USAID is working with many other agencies to develop plans to improve the financial sector transparency, reform the energy sector and improve the operating environment for private sector businesses.

Mr. Chairman, Mr. Engel, members of the committee, thank you for this opportunity to testify on the issues of great importance, not only for Ukraine but for the region and for the United States.

This is a critical moment for an opportunity for Ukraine and USAID is well positioned to help Ukraine meet some of its most pressing challenges, and as my colleagues have noted, the IMF will be crucial to those efforts.

This concludes my testimony. I am prepared for questions.

[The prepared statement of Ms. Alexander follows:]

**Statement of Paige E. Alexander**
**Assistant Administrator, Bureau for Europe and Eurasia**
**U.S. Agency for International Development**
**Before the**
**House Committee on Foreign Affairs**
**"U.S. Foreign Policy Toward Ukraine"**
**March 6, 2014**

Mr. Chairman, Ranking Member Engel, distinguished Members of the Committee, thank you for inviting me to testify before you today regarding United States assistance for the people of Ukraine.

Recent events are momentous for Ukraine and the response of the United States government is critical to the region's future. The U.S. is working with our international partners -- especially the International Monetary Fund -- to provide needed support to Ukraine's people and economy as they face the current crisis. Our approach is to support the goals and aspirations of all of the people of Ukraine for peace, prosperity, freedom, and human dignity -- the very things that so many Ukrainians were demanding on the Maidan.

Elections are less than three months away and support is needed first and foremost to ensure that they are free, fair, transparent, and inclusive. Successful elections will be essential to demonstrate to the world and to the Ukrainian people that Ukraine is on a democratic path.

At the same time, years of economic mismanagement have left Ukraine with an uncompetitive business climate and overvalued exchange rate. Ukraine's energy sector continues to be a significant drain on Ukraine's financial resources and has left Ukraine highly dependent on imported gas. Ukraine urgently needs to implement economic reforms, with the support of the IMF, to restore economic stability and avert a financial crisis, which would further undermine stability and make progress in other areas impossible.

The people of Ukraine, on the Maidan and throughout the country, are demanding an end to official corruption, including insider dealings and misappropriation of funds by government officials. The new government has made a pledge to do this, and early indications are promising that they will take serious action.

Against this backdrop, the U.S. package of bilateral assistance that was announced on Tuesday is focused on meeting Ukraine's most pressing needs and helping

Ukraine to make needed reforms in the medium and long-term. We as a government are focused on four areas: implementing critical economic reforms; promoting free, fair, inclusive and peaceful elections, with robust involvement by a strong and independent civil society and media; combatting corruption and recovering stolen assets; and assisting Ukraine in withstanding politically motivated trade actions by Russia.

On economic reforms, we will work to complement Ukraine's work with the IMF to implement the reforms needed to put the country on a more sound economic footing in the medium and long-term. Addressing these challenges will require implementation of economic reforms that can restore Ukraine to economic health. Only the IMF can provide the needed technical expertise, reassurance to markets, and large-scale financing needed to stabilize the Ukrainian economy and avert a debilitating financial crisis. We will use our bilateral assistance to make the success of an IMF program more likely, by providing technical assistance to support reforms and to soften their impact on vulnerable Ukrainian households.

U.S. technical assistance in these areas will be critical to helping Ukraine return to economic stability and growth and move forward on its democratic path. We need to assist the Ukrainian people in addressing these challenges and promote a path to sustainable long-term economic development. Failure to do so would risk undermining our policy efforts. We also need to revitalize support to the private sector, which has stagnated in recent years because of an increasingly uneven playing field and official harassment. Complex bureaucracy and low wages for many law enforcement and other public sector officials create added opportunity for corruption. USAID is working with other agencies to develop plans to improve financial sector transparency, reform the energy sector, and improve the operating environment for private business.

We will also work with you to pass 2010 IMF quota legislation, which would support the IMF's capacity to lend additional resources to Ukraine, while also helping to preserve continued U.S. leadership within this important institution.

On promoting free and fair elections, specifically, we will work to improve the legal framework and strengthen election administration. The new government is poised to enact necessary reforms of election legislation in the short term. Our efforts will facilitate inclusive dialogue, technical assistance, and civil society engagement on electoral law reform. We will also provide technical assistance to the Central Election Commission for the training of election management bodies and officials, and on voter education.

We plan to support international and domestic election observation. Broad and diversified oversight of the electoral process is critical for ensuring transparency and thus the legitimacy of these elections. Local and international elections watchdog organizations have played a highly constructive role in past elections in Ukraine, and additional support for them will help establish both domestic and international legitimacy of the results.

Additional support is required for more comprehensive long- and short-term observation missions. We will help support both a domestic non-governmental group and a coalition of regional non-governmental election monitoring organizations. We're coordinating closely with State's European Bureau and the Bureau of Democracy, Human Rights, and Labor on supporting robust electoral oversight. We will also support a high-level pre-election assessment and Election Day missions from the National Democratic Institute and the International Republican Institute that can leverage their decades-long, global experience in election monitoring.

We will work to harness the constructive energy generated by the EuroMaidan movement, and we will support civil society coalition building to advocate for further reform. Through consultations, training, and new technology, our longstanding elections and political processes implementing partners can help political parties be more responsive to citizens and strengthen relationships with civil society. They can also assist parties and alliances emerging from the EuroMaidan movement to organize and participate constructively in the elections. Additional support will include training for party poll-watchers and additional public opinion polling on voter attitudes.

We will also work to support independent media outlets to help promote a more open and diverse information environment throughout the country, including media monitoring during the campaign. We will support investigative journalists working to help combat corruption and assist in the recovery of stolen assets. We plan to help the Government of Ukraine create more robust safeguards against corruption and recover assets stolen from the people of Ukraine in accordance with the rule of law.

On addressing corruption, a majority of Ukraine's citizens have made clear to the world their desire for a more open, democratic, and accountable form of governance – one that represents its people, that is not corrupt and that operates transparently. We plan to help the Government of Ukraine create more robust safeguards against corruption and recover assets stolen from the people of Ukraine.

We have long supported the work of Ukrainian organizations advocating for respect for human rights, and we plan to continue assisting them, including those that have emerged as leaders in monitoring of recent human rights violations and advocating for universal human values.

In addition to these immediate needs, we also recognize that the creation of more inclusive and accountable government takes more than just one election. Ukraine has vibrant and multi-faceted civil society, which is both authentically indigenous and has also benefited from our sustained support through the years since independence. Mid-range and longer term needs will include the further strengthening of civil society and independent media, efforts to help the government engage more fully and substantively with all sectors of society, a continued focus on anti-corruption measures, continued support for parliamentary strengthening and development, renewed reform of the judicial system, and a consideration of reasonable steps towards de-centralization.

In the health sector for instance Ukrainians face corruption on a daily basis. Such corruption has led to high prices of pharmaceuticals and to serious shortages of childhood vaccines. Partly as a result, Ukraine is now facing an immediate and serious threat of a polio outbreak. Inflated drug prices have also led to shortages in anti-retroviral drugs for HIV patients. Previously the U.S. Government has enjoyed strong cooperation with the people of Ukraine in the health sector that has helped reduce maternal and infant morbidity. Now the government's commitment to fight corruption and reform the health system provides USAID with an opportunity to provide targeted assistance in improving health systems and immunization rates and restoring public confidence in the health system.

Mr. Chairman, Mr. Engel, members of the Committee, thank you again for this opportunity to testify on this issue of great importance, not only for Ukraine, but for the region, and for the United States. This is a critical moment of opportunity for Ukraine and USAID is well poised to help Ukraine meet some of its most pressing challenges. And, as my colleagues have noted, the IMF will be crucial to our efforts. This concludes my prepared testimony, and I am prepared to answer any questions you may have.

Chairman ROYCE. Thanks, Ms. Alexander.
We will go immediately to Mr. Singh.

## STATEMENT OF MR. DALEEP SINGH, DEPUTY ASSISTANT SEC-RETARY FOR EUROPE AND EURASIA, U.S. DEPARTMENT OF THE TREASURY

Mr. SINGH. Chairman Royce, Ranking Member Engel and members of the committee, thank you for the opportunity to  testify today.

I visited Kiev last week to meet with government officials and express our solidarity during this difficult moment.

Secretary Lew has spoken several times with the Ukrainian Prime Minister, who has assured us that the government is prepared to take the necessary steps to build a secure economic foundation, including the implementation of urgently needed reforms to restore financial stability, unleash economic potential and promote the economic aspirations of the Ukrainian people.

The fragility of Ukraine's financial condition underscores the urgency of its new government committing to an IMF-led reform program and securing the financing it needs while difficult adjustments are made.

The fragile economic situation in Ukraine stems from many years of poor policy choices, lack of reform and corruption under previous governments as well as the negative confidence effect from Russia's recent actions in Crimea.

Ukraine's new leadership has declared publicly and committed privately its willingness to undertake the necessary steps to secure assistance from the IMF and others, and the United  States  has made clear that as Ukraine implements reforms we will work with our partners to support the Ukrainian people and restore the country's economic and political stability.

As part of this international effort, the United States has developed a package of bilateral assistance funded primarily by a loan guarantee that is focused on meeting Ukraine's most pressing needs. These efforts will complement what must be the centerpiece of an international assistance effort and IMF program.

Only the IMF has the capacity to provide the necessary large-scale resources and the expertise to design and support a reform agenda in Ukraine. An IMF program also sends the strongest signal of confidence to markets, businesses and households at a time when sentiment remains volatile.

More specifically, the IMF has the expertise to develop in consultation with Ukrainian authorities an economic adjustment program that eliminates unsustainable economic imbalances, removes costly and poorly-targeted government subsidies and improves Ukraine's business climate and competitiveness.

The central role of the IMF in this assistance effort is an illustration of why the IMF is so vital to U.S. economic and political interests.

The IMF is the world's first and most active responder in an economic crisis. By providing financial support and hands-on policy advice, the IMF helps keep our allies and partners strong and prevents economic dissatisfaction from spiraling into political instability. This makes the IMF's role critical to our nation's economic well being.

When instability abroad washes up on our shores, lower U.S. growth results in fewer jobs and our citizens' savings and 401Ks are hurt through financial markets.

For the United States to continue playing a leading role at the IMF as it helps Ukraine, one of the most significant steps we can take right now is to pass the 2010 IMF quota and governance reforms.

Why is this so important? First, the United States is the only major economy that has not passed the 2010 quota reforms and our inability to act has led other countries to worry that the United States is retreating from its position of leadership at the IMF at a time when its role is so pivotal to the future of Ukraine.

Second, the quota reforms would support the IMF's capacity to lend additional resources to Ukraine if it needs bridge financing to a larger package. We should be in favor of providing as much financial flexibility and resources as possible to the IMF in support of Ukraine's financial stability.

There exists broad support in the American business community for these IMF reforms. The U.S. Chamber of Commerce, Financial Services Roundtable, Securities Industry and Financial Markets Association, Financial Service Forum and Business Roundtable all agree that these changes are necessary and in the best interest of American businesses and the global economy.

Part of the reason why the business community supports these reforms is that it is a safe and smart investment for the United States. The legislation will not add one new dollar to overall commitment to the IMF.

The IMF has a rock solid balance sheet with liquid reserves and gold holdings that exceed all of its credit outstanding. The IMF has never defaulted on any U.S. Reserve claims on the IMF since its inception 70 years ago.

If we fail to pass the 2010 quota reforms, our voice may diminish and we will miss an opportunity to bolster the fund's resources and economies may turn away from the IMF toward regionalism, bilateral arrangements or new institutions, which means that the United States will lose the leverage and influence it has built up over decades at a time when our leadership on the global stage is so critical.

Chairman Royce, Ranking Member Engel, members of the committee, Ukraine has asked for our support during this difficult time and the United States, along with its partners, should be ready to answer the call.

Thank you.

[The prepared statement of Mr. Singh follows:]

***EMBARGOED FOR DELIVERY***

**Testimony of Daleep Singh, Deputy Assistant Secretary for Europe & Eurasia
before the House Foreign Affairs Committee**
March 6, 2014

## Introduction

Chairman Royce, Ranking Member Engel, and members of the committee, thank you for the opportunity to testify today.

The U.S. Treasury is carefully monitoring the situation in Ukraine, and we are coordinating closely with our counterparts in Europe and the international financial institutions. I visited Kyiv last week and met with government officials to discuss the latest developments and to express our support during this difficult moment. Secretary Lew has spoken several times with the Ukrainian Prime Minister, who has assured us that the government is prepared to take the necessary steps to build a secure economic foundation, including urgently needed reforms to restore financial stability, unleash economic potential, and allow Ukraine's people to better achieve their economic aspirations. The fragility of Ukraine's financial condition underscores the urgency of its new government committing to an IMF-led reform program and securing the financing it needs while necessary economic adjustments are made.

## Economic Situation

The economic situation in Ukraine is quite fragile – stemming from many years of unsustainable economic policies under previous governments, as well as the negative confidence impact from Russia's recent actions in Crimea. Deposit withdrawals from banks have accelerated in recent weeks and Ukraine's currency – the hyrvnia – has experienced marked pressure, prompting the central bank to cease defending the fixed-exchange rate and to impose administrative controls. Without access to international capital markets and with limited foreign exchange reserves to repay maturing debt and purchase imports, Ukraine's new government has requested official assistance from the IMF and signaled a commitment to economic reforms in order to avoid intensification of the current crisis.

Extensive state involvement in the economy continues to hinder growth and investment, and Ukraine's recovery from the global financial crisis of 2008 – which hit Ukraine especially hard as GDP fell by 15 percent – lags well behind its peers. Tight credit conditions and foreign exchange controls in support of Ukraine's managed exchange rate have constrained business activity and exacerbated existing vulnerabilities to external shocks. A difficult business climate impairs private sector development, as weak property rights, corruption, and an inefficient legal system deter investment and hinder economic growth. And despite one of the highest average costs of gas supply in Europe, Ukraine's residential gas and heating tariffs are among the lowest in the region. These large, poorly-targeted energy subsidies contribute to unsustainable government deficits and, perhaps most significantly, underinvestment in Ukraine's domestic energy sector – ultimately increasing Ukraine's dependence on Russian natural gas and vulnerability to Russian influence. The IMF and World Bank have estimated that overall energy subsidies cost roughly 7 percent of GDP in 2012, with relatively well-off households capturing the larger share of benefits.

Taken together, the lack of progress tackling much-needed reforms in these segments of the economy continues to prevent Ukraine, from realizing its full potential. As such, Ukraine was stuck in recession for much of 2013, and the outlook for 2014 and beyond has deteriorated significantly in light of recent events.

In response to the evolving crisis in Ukraine, we have been working closely with international partners to develop a coordinated assistance package that will help the Ukrainian government implement the reforms needed to restore financial stability and economic growth. Ukraine's new government has declared publicly its commitment to undertake the necessary steps to secure assistance from the IMF and others, and the United States has made clear that as Ukraine undertakes meaningful reforms, we stand ready to work with our partners to provide the support needed to avoid a further deterioration of the situation in Ukraine.

**International Assistance Package**

An international assistance package to Ukraine would be centered around an IMF program, as only the IMF has the capacity and expertise to help Ukraine develop a comprehensive adjustment program. In exchange for implementation of credible macroeconomic reform commitments, the IMF can provide significant financing to meet Ukraine's needs and set the economy on sound footing. At the request of Ukraine's new government, an IMF mission team is currently in Kyiv working with the Ukrainian authorities to assess the country's economic and financing needs.

Any IMF-based support package can be complemented by assistance from multilateral development banks such as the World Bank and European Bank for Reconstruction and Development (EBRD), which stand ready and willing to support Ukraine. Together, the World Bank and EBRD can provide additional financial and technical support to achieve energy sector and social safety net reforms while easing the impact of necessary economic reforms on Ukraine's most vulnerable individuals. Additionally, our partners in the European Union have expressed their intention to provide significant bilateral support to Ukraine should the government take the steps to implement robust, market-oriented reforms.

As part of this international effort, the United States has developed a package of bilateral assistance focused on meeting Ukraine's four most pressing needs: (1) implementing critical economic reforms and cushioning their impact on vulnerable Ukrainians; (2) conducting successful elections and strengthening independent media and civil society; (3) combating corruption and recovering stolen assets; and (4) withstanding politically motivated trade actions by Russia.

Specifically, we are seeking Congressional authorization to provide the Government of Ukraine with sovereign loan guarantees for up to $1 billion in Ukrainian borrowing, the proceeds of which could be used to protect poor Ukrainian households from the impact of required economic adjustments. Also, we are asking that Congress approve IMF quota legislation, which would support the IMF's capacity to lend additional resources to Ukraine while also helping to preserve continued U.S. leadership within this important institution.

The United States is also moving quickly to deploy a range of other financing and technical expertise, including providing highly experienced technical advisors to help the Ukrainian financial authorities manage immediate market pressures and support Ukraine as it negotiates with the IMF.

**IMF Quota Reform**

The United States stands ready to support Ukraine as it undertakes the economic reforms it needs to return to stability. But, as I've mentioned here today, U.S. bilateral assistance must be accompanied by an IMF program to succeed in restoring Ukraine's economic health. Only the IMF has the capacity to provide the necessary large-scale resources, ability to restore market confidence, and capacity to design and support reforms in countries facing large-scale economic vulnerabilities, such as Ukraine.

The IMF is the world's first responder in a financial crisis: by providing financial support and hands-on policy advice, the IMF helps keep our allies and partners strong. In emerging economies such as Ukraine, the IMF can help provide needed financing and policy advice. The IMF works in fragile states alongside multilateral development banks to combat economic stagnation and dissatisfaction, which can give rise to political instability and extremism.

More specifically, the IMF has the expertise to develop, in consultation with the Ukrainian authorities, an economic adjustment program that eliminates unsustainable economic imbalances, removes costly and poorly targeted government subsidies, and improves Ukraine's business climate and competitiveness in order to unleash Ukraine's latent economic potential. Without the economic stability that only the IMF can provide to Ukraine, progress on much needed, long-overdue structural reforms will continue to lag – much to the detriment of the 45 million people who call Ukraine home and yearn for a better future.

For the United States to continue playing a leading role in international support efforts for Ukraine, centered on the IMF, one of the most significant steps we can take is to pass the 2010 IMF quota and governance reforms. As I mentioned, passage of this legislation would support the IMF's capacity to lend additional resources to Ukraine, while also helping to preserve continued U.S. leadership within this important institution. Approving these reforms puts the United States in a stronger position to exercise leadership at the IMF on a host of issues critical to our economic and national security.

There exists broad support in the American business community for these IMF reforms. The U.S. Chamber of Commerce, Financial Service Roundtable, Securities Industry and Financial Markets Association (SIFMA), Financial Service Forum, and Business Roundtable all agree that these changes are necessary and in the best interest of American businesses and the global economy. Likewise, a bipartisan group of former senior government officials at the Bretton Woods Committee has written to Congress urging support of these long-overdue reforms – emphasizing that a stronger IMF, driven by U.S. leadership, supports U.S. and global interests.

The IMF is a vital tool in our national security toolkit. The Fund's efforts to promote economic and financial stability across the globe often impact countries where greater instability would otherwise be harmful to U.S. global interests. The Fund's response to support nations impacted by the Arab Spring such as Jordan, Tunisia, and Yemen are a few examples. Needless to say, the IMF is critical to our nation's economic wellbeing – when instability abroad washes up on our shores, lower U.S. growth results in fewer jobs and exports, and our citizens' savings and 401Ks are hit through financial contagion.

The IMF is a safe and smart investment for the United States, with a rock solid balance sheet including reserves and gold holdings that exceed total IMF credit outstanding (about $127 billion). In addition, the IMF is recognized by its entire membership as the preferred creditor, with the unique ability to set conditions to assure repayment. The IMF has never defaulted on any U.S. reserve claims on the IMF since its inception nearly 70 years ago.

And the IMF has protected U.S. economic and security interests by helping many of our closest partners get back on their feet.

But if, as a result of our failure to pass the 2010 quota reforms, emerging economies turn away from the IMF toward regionalism, bilateral arrangements, or new institutions, the United States will lose the leverage and influence it has built up over decades through the IMF and its central role in anchoring countries in the multilateral system – influence which is vitally important as seen by ongoing events in Ukraine and Russia.

The United States is the last major economy that has yet to pass the 2010 quota reform and our approval is the only remaining step for these long-delayed important reforms to go into effect. Our failure to act has led other countries to worry that the United States is retreating from our leadership role at the IMF, and the Administration is actively working to include the 2010 IMF quota reform in any Ukraine legislation.

**Conclusion**

Chairman Royce, Ranking Member Engel, and members of the committee: Ukraine has asked for support from the international community during this difficult time and the United States, in partnership with the IMF, the World Bank, EBRD, and our allies in Europe, is ready to answer their call. We must continue to play a leading role in supporting Ukraine, both bilaterally and through the IMF. We can take an important first step at this critical time by providing support for our proposed loan guarantee and bilateral assistance and passing the 2010 IMF quota reform as part of any Ukraine assistance package.

———

Chairman ROYCE. Thank you, Daleep.

In the interests of allowing our newer members of this committee to ask any questions and get information that they need, I am going to forego my time and pass to Mr. Engel of New York.

Mr. ENGEL. Thank you, Mr. Chairman, and I am going to only ask one question to give more people an opportunity to ask questions. I think I am going to ask it to you, Mr. Rubin.

Russia has exerted intense pressure, especially economically, on Ukraine in the past and my fear is that Ukraine can expect more pressure in the months ahead.

So how can we and our European allies help Ukraine and other countries such as Moldova and Georgia, which are attempting to build democratic states, resist this pressure?

One of the things that worried me about leading to this crisis is that Putin, in trying to lure these countries into his customs union, offers them all kinds of goodies, bonuses, gas, money, and the European Union says well, we would like you to affiliate with us in an Eastern partnership but there are 12 hoops you first have to jump through, and then if you jump through them and land on your feet we will consider you.

I really think that the playing field has not been leveled and we create obstacles to having these countries join with us to look westward rather than eastward. They all complain to me when they come in to my office, and what can we do to change this?

Mr. RUBIN. Thank you. I would like to first talk about the economic aspects of your question and I think I can point to some recent action both on the part of the European Union and the United States to address the very concerns you are talking about, Congressman.

I think most importantly I would like to talk about the emergency assistance that we have announced, that the European Union has announced, which is tied in with the key reforms that the Ukrainian Government needs to make to get its economy back on its feet.

The European Union announced a major package this week and Secretary Kerry in Kiev announced that we are starting to put together a package that will include a $1 billion loan guarantee that we have already been consulting with members on the Hill about, including this committee.

And I think it is very important to recognize the perilous financial situation that Ukraine finds itself in under Russian pressure but also under very serious previous mismanagement and bad economic policy.

The new government has taken a very encouraging and promising set of steps and we believe that the new government is very serious about moving quickly to get Ukraine back on its feet.

It needs support. We are committed to providing that support starting with not just the loan guarantee that we are talking about but increased technical assistance and other forms of aid, and then, most importantly, working together with our allies and partners so that it is the international community that is supporting Ukraine with the United States as the leading part of that effort.

Moldova and Georgia are very vulnerable as well, there is no question, and we have been working very, very closely with their governments.

We had the Prime Minister of Georgia here 2 weeks ago at the White House, meeting with President Obama, Vice President Biden, the Prime Minister of Moldova last Monday also meeting with the President, the Vice President, the Secretary of State.

We are working to do everything we can to help them financially but also to provide the critical public and political support for the democratic choices of their people, and we will be doing that in the months ahead.

But I think it is very important that basically underlying the point that this is a critical moment to give them that support now when you have governments that are making the right choices.

We recognize that. We will be doing that.

Chairman ROYCE. Eric, you are a little too close to that mike. Just move it back a little bit.

Ileana Ros-Lehtinen of Florida.

Ms. ROS-LEHTINEN. Thank you so much, Mr. Chairman, for calling this hearing and for your excellent bill. The Magnitsky list— that is what I wanted to ask about.

Denying and revoking visas of Russian regime members who are connected to belligerent actions in Ukraine and freezing and prohibiting any of their U.S. property transactions are moves in the right direction.

But now we must name and shame these persons, add them and other Putin officials responsible for human rights abuses not just in Ukraine but in Russia as well to the Magnitsky list, which imposes similar sanctions.

Adding these names to the Magnitsky list would make these sanctions permanent rather than an Executive order that the President can rescind.

I have already submitted many names to the Obama administration to add to that list since we passed the Magnitsky Act and there are many names here—names, position, examples and evidence of gross human rights violations.

I will send a new letter to the administration asking for more names of human rights violators to be added to the Magnitsky list and I hope that my colleagues will join me in that letter.

And the President must take similar actions in Venezuela where Maduro continues his suppression of the people who seek freedom and democracy. In the Executive order of the President he talks about actions or policies that undermine democratic process or institutions in Ukraine.

Well, Maduro and his officials are also responsible for actions and policies that undermine democratic processes or institutions in Venezuela, and now is the time to act. Sixteen of my colleagues sent a letter to the President asking for those similar powers under the International Emergency Economic Powers Act.

So, Mr. Rubin, my question to you is, is the administration considering adding more names of Russian officials guilty of human rights violations to the Magnitsky list?

Is it simply a historical document for academics to ponder? Are we just going to stay with those few names that we have put on the list and have not added many since then?

Mr. RUBIN. Thank you, Congresswoman Ros-Lehtinen.

We are actively considering adding new names. The answer to your question is, absolutely, we take the legislation very seriously, and I do not have any new information for you this morning but that is something that is under active consideration.

Ms. ROS-LEHTINEN. Thank you, sir.

Chairman ROYCE. Thank you.

Gregory Meeks from New York.

Mr. MEEKS. Thank you, Mr. Chairman.

Let me just see if I can do a real quick question. First, Mr. Singh, I know that the Treasury Department is working closely with the Department of State and the White House on a loan guarantee package for the Ukraine, and you talked about it briefly in your opening statement.

But I was wondering if you can discuss in more detail how we in Congress can support and improve the capacity of the IMF to provide a guaranteed loan package.

Mr. SINGH. Thank you for your question, Congressman.

So the IMF, in any assistance package for Ukraine that is going to be credible, needs to play a central role and the best thing we can do right now is to maintain our leading voice at the institution, the IMF, that is going to be at the heart of the assistance effort.

If we don't meet our basic commitments to fund the IMF and pass the quota reforms our voice may diminish. Now, there is a second reason.

Passing the quota reform provides the IMF with more financing flexibility, particularly in the case where Ukraine could need a bridge—a short-term assistance package—as a means to get to a larger agreement with the IMF.

Now, the IMF is on the ground, are looking at the data. We don't know yet whether that flexibility will be needed. But it is a good idea to have it.

Mr. MEEKS. Thank you.

Ms. Alexander, as you prepare for the long-term engagement in development in the Ukraine, are you confident that the interim Ukrainian Government is a stable partner for USAID?

Ms. ALEXANDER. Thank you, Congressman Meeks.

The benefit of the people that we have worked with in Ukraine is that one of the development assets that Ukraine has is also its vibrant multifaceted civil society.

So we not only work with the Ukrainian Government, we work directly with civil society. But we have been very impressed with what we have seen in the Ukrainian Government thus far. We have been impressed with their restraint and we consider them good partners.

So we are confident that our money will be well spent.

Mr. MEEKS. And finally, Mr. Rubin, I am a firm believer in multilateralism in a multilateral way and I think it is vitally important for the United States to do that and to have this unified voice toward Russia for their action in Ukraine.

How can the United States—I think this is something I just want you to elaborate a little bit more—better engage our allies in Europe to ensure that we have the same strategic goals and long-term planning for continued development and prosperity of the U.S.-European relationship? It seems there have been some cracks recently.

Mr. RUBIN. Well, thank you, Congressman.

We have actually made this a very high priority and Secretary Kerry has spent the past 2 days in Europe, in Rome and Paris following his visit to Kiev working precisely on that—working with our allies and other interested governments to try to craft a united international community approach to supporting Ukraine to ending this conflict, to convincing Russia to withdraw its troops and restore its recognition of Ukraine's sovereignty and territorial integrity.

We agree that this needs to be a collective international approach. It needs to be a diplomatic approach.

We believe that the call of the international community for this to be settled through dialogue, for Russia and Ukraine to immediately begin talking about this can only happen if the international community is united in supporting this and that is precisely what the Secretary is in Europe doing right now.

Chairman ROYCE. Chris Smith of New Jersey.

Mr. SMITH. Thank you, Mr. Chairman.

Mr. Rubin, how do you assess the risk of escalation by miscalculation? With so many AK–47s pointing at each other, only one troop or one soldier has to fire and things could get out of hand.

You mentioned the OSCE monitors. They have been stopped. As you know, they can't get in. When I have visited OSCE monitors in other countries including Georgia, Croatia, and elsewhere over the years, they have such limited capabilities to mitigate a firefight or any kind of hostility.

Secondly, I was in Tbilisi, Georgia a few days after the Russians rolled in to Abkhazia and South Ossetia. They several times put their tanks on a road as if they were going into Tbilisi, only to turn around.

You will recall that. Their objective strategically was Abkhazia and South Ossetia. What is the objective of the Russians now?

Is it just Crimea or are other regions and cities in Ukraine, particularly in the eastern area, in the cross hairs? And Mr. Singh, if you could, Sergei Glazyev has said that Russia will abandon the U.S. dollar as a reserve currency if the U.S. initiates sanctions against Russia.

How seriously do we take that threat? Sanctions now have been levied, as they ought to be, and the Eurasia Economic Union had a meeting this week with Belarus, Kazakhstan, and Putin talking about that union that comes into force in 2015. How does that play into all of this?

Mr. RUBIN. Thank you, Congressman.

The question of international observers and monitors is absolutely critical, as you stated. We believe that the best way to de-escalate this very dangerous conflict to ensure that there are no accidental incidents that lead to escalation is to have an international

29

presence, eyes and ears on the ground, and that is what we have been supporting.

That is what the OSCE has been supporting. That is what the special envoy of the United Nations Secretary-General is there for.

We believe that they need access to all areas of Ukraine. They have access to all areas except Crimea. The Ukranian Government has been very supportive in encouraging monitors to come in to address any allegations of abuses, to address any concerns about minority rights and that is the way to address these concerns is through eyes and ears on the ground that can provide an objective assessment of what is going on and also be there as witnesses to what is going on.

We find the fact that the monitors have had extreme difficulty in getting into Crimea and performing their activities in Crimea is very worrying.

It is something that we consider unacceptable and we believe that all the authorities involved including the local authorities have an absolute obligation to allow that to happen and we will be pushing to expand the monitoring.

We will be pushing to expand the scope of the monitoring and without that we fear it will be very hard to actually know what is going on. To answer your question as to what the Russians' objectives are, I have to say I think we all wish we knew the answer to that question.

We have seen that, clearly, one objective is to militarily occupy and control the territory of the autonomous region of Crimea. We have condemned that. We consider it unacceptable. We believe the Russian forces must return to their barracks under their treaty obligations in the basin treaty with Ukraine.

We certainly would condemn any further use of Russian military force or aggression on the territory of Ukraine. We hope that we will not see any further use and that we can return to a diplomatic dialogue to end this very, very unfortunate situation.

And with that, let me turn to Mr. Singh.

Chairman ROYCE. The reserve currency portion of it, Mr. Singh.

Mr. SINGH. Yes. Congressman, let me give you a simple answer. Russia doesn't get to decide the world reserve currencies or the United States level of interest rates. That is determined by our economic outlook and our monetary policy.

We have the most deep and liquid capital markets. We have the most attractive investment environment. This is not—we control our own destiny in this regard, not Russia.

Chairman ROYCE. We go to Albio Sires from New Jersey.

Mr. SIRES. Thank you, Mr. Chairman, and thank the members that are here today.

You know, I certainly believe that we should have strong sanctions. I don't think Putin understands anything else. But how can we get strong sanctions when Europe over the last few years has become more and more dependent on energy from Russia? And, for example, Germany didn't jump right away because obviously, we think it is something like 40 percent of the gas from Russia.

So how can we get a consensus to come up with strong sanctions against Russia when they are so dependent? So and the other question that I have is Russia is threatening that if strong sanctions start to impact their economy they are going to go after the assets that we have in Russia—our American assets.

What are we prepared to do if they go after those companies and American assets in Russia?

Mr. RUBIN. Thank you, Congressman.

Let me address, first, the question of coordinating sanctions policy with our allies and partners. The European Council of the European Union yesterday issued a very comprehensive framework for imposing sanctions and the leaders of the nations of the European Union are meeting today to consider that.

We believe that our allies and partners in Europe understand the seriousness of this. We have been working very closely with them including Secretary Kerry's meetings throughout the past 2 days in Paris and Rome and we agree with you that there needs to be a coordinated international approach to make clear to the Russian federation that there will be serious consequences for Russia, for the Russian economy, for Russia's standing in the world if Russia continues its current course of action.

This is not intended as a threat. This is not intended as any form of economic coercion on anyone's part. This is intended to say that the international community is based on a set of principles, a set of laws of the United Nations Charter, the Helsinki Final Act—all of the obligations that members have toward each other and it must be followed.

That is the basic foundation of the international system and of the post-war settlement in Europe. So this is simply a clear message to Russia that Russia has to return to respecting those norms, those commitments, those laws.

We believe that there will be coordinated international action, that it will not be just the United States imposing sanctions and other forms in response to Russia's actions. We believe we will see that very shortly and we will work very hard to ensure that this is a coordinated international front.

I would add just to say that we will very strongly support the rights of our companies, our investors and the basic principles of international law and all the other obligations that countries have toward foreign investors and we take that obligation very seriously.

Mr. SIRES. Mr. Singh, can you address the issue of——

Mr. SINGH. Sure. Congressman, Mr. Rubin is right. We are working very closely with our European counterparts.

But the reality is, you know, Russia is a—it is a very large economy. It is a $2 trillion economy, eighth largest in the world.

There are interconnections on the trade front, on the financial front, on the market front. It is important that we are proportionate in our response, depending on Russia's actions.

With respect to the energy question in particular, I would just observe there is a—there is a co-dependence. Yes, Europe relies—you know, roughly a third of their energy imports come from Russia but so too does depend on those earnings—on those export earnings to Europe. And so they also need to be careful.

Mr. SIRES. Thank you, Mr. Chairman.

Chairman ROYCE. We go to Mr. Steve Chabot of Ohio.

Mr. CHABOT. Thank you, Mr. Chairman.

President Putin's recent explanations for his aggressive actions in Crimea don't pass the laugh test. Putin suggests that he is obligated to protect his fellow Russians in Ukraine when, in fact, Crimea was last part of the old Soviet Union back in 1956. I was 3 years old when it became part of Ukraine and remained so after the fall of the Soviet Union and the advent of an independent Ukraine in 1991.

His arguments are weak and his actions are, clearly, in violation of international law. But, unfortunately, there is the perception, at least, that there is a growing power vacuum around the world and various bad actors are filling it from the Middle East, the South China Sea, now to Ukraine.

In the last few weeks, we heard from the White House about consequences, all options on the table, and so forth. It wasn't that long ago, my colleagues will remember, that we were hearing about drawing a line in the sand and, frankly, I fear that there may be a growing perception among our friends and allies in the international community that the United States, at least in the area of foreign policy, lacks resolve.

So I hope our witnesses this morning will be able to alleviate some of those concerns. A couple of questions—where are we in regards to our cooperative efforts with our European partners? I have heard some vague comments about consequences from European officials. How serious are they? Who are the players in the region that are working closest with us and where are the weak links?

It has been suggested that some of our allies in Europe would never agree to strong sanctions on Russia because of the fear that their sources of energy supplies would be cut off. Well, here is an idea: Perhaps our friends in Europe would be able to avoid that fate if they in fact produced more of their own energy, which is present but untapped because of their own domestic energy policies, which we encourage. Or even better, the Obama administration could reverse its anti-production policies. Approve the Keystone Pipeline, for example and open up ANWR. If we encourage the development of our shale export program, the Europeans could buy their energy from us while increasing American manufacturing jobs. Just a thought.

I have given you a lot to think about. Any comments?

Mr. RUBIN. Congressman, thank you.

Let me say that in terms of assuring that we have unity of purpose and action with our allies and partners in Europe, this is our highest priority. Again, this has been the main objective of Secretary Kerry's work in the past several days in Europe.

We believe we have seen clear statements that the leaders of the European Union, of the European Union's member states and of countries in Europe that are not members of the European Union are very serious about the threat that this set of developments poses will take action and we are working very hard to coordinate our action with them so that we are presenting a strong coordinated front on this.

Let me also say that we have seen action taken by countries not in the European Union and countries in the European Union already to impose sanctions to freeze accounts, to take other steps, visa bans, to make clear that there will be consequences for a violation of the international order.

Additionally, let me mention that it is our highest priority to ensure that the solemn commitments that we have under the North Atlantic Treaty to our allies in Europe are upheld.

We take that obligation with the utmost seriousness. We have worked within NATO in the past several days to ensure that we are prepared within the alliance to support all its members.

We have taken action to expand our Baltic air policing mission, our aviation detachment in Poland. The North Atlantic Council issued a very strong statement on behalf of all the allies and we will be working very closely with them in coming days and weeks to ensure that the alliance stands strong and united on this.

The last point that you mentioned, I would just like to say that energy diversification has been at the heart of our policy toward Europe for the past 25 years under every administration and it remains at the heart of that.

Obviously, there is still a long way to go but we strongly believe that diverse sources of energy, lack of reliance on a single supplier, is very important for Europe's security and future development.

Thank you.

Chairman ROYCE. We go now to Mr. Brian Higgins of New York. Or did you have a point you wanted to make, Mr. Singh?

Mr. SINGH. I was just going to make the point that it is clearly important to collaborate closely on sanctions but we should also acknowledge a very welcome announcement by Europe yesterday in terms of their assistance to the Ukrainian people.

And what is important right now is that we all come together as an international community and meet Ukraine's financing needs as it makes the reforms it needs to achieve economic stability which will pave the path to an independent political future.

Chairman ROYCE. Thank you. Mr. Higgins.

Mr. HIGGINS. Thank you, Mr. Chairman.

Russia has violated all kinds of international laws including the treaty they signed with Ukraine guaranteeing its borders in return for which Ukraine gave up its nuclear weapons.

Russia's occupation of Ukraine is a direct and clear violation of Ukraine's sovereignty and territorial integrity. President Putin has acted like a international street thug, and in 1994 when Russia was included into the G–8 it was a recognition that the post-Soviet Russia was behaving like an honorable member of the international community and not a rogue state.

If Russia's behavior has changed then it would seem to me that Russia's status as a member of the G–8 should change a little bit more aggressively than simply a suspension. Their membership should be revoked. It should be revoked.

Number two—NATO, which is 28 countries including the United States and Canada and 26 European countries, was essentially established to safeguard the freedom and security through political and military means.

It was a vehicle through which democratic principles could be promoted. Any thoughts about the idea of permanently kicking Russia out of the G–8 and offering membership to the—to Ukraine in NATO?

Mr. RUBIN. Thank you, Congressman.

As the White House announcement stated this morning, we have suspended all preparations for attending the G–8 summit in Sochi, and as we have said previously it is hard to imagine that the President would go under current circumstances.

The larger question you ask, obviously, is something that the President will need to consider and I think this gets to the bigger picture question, which is Russia's role in the world, how Russia participates as a member of the international community under the structures and laws and obligations that all members of the international community have toward each other.

So I think the larger question is very clear. We, as I mentioned, take the North Atlantic Alliance and its obligations solemnly, seriously and we are looking actively to consider how we can do more as an alliance to respond to this set of developments.

But I would also add that we have said all along that the alliance is based on a set of values and commitments and principles what kind of societies have come together and in this case we have stated publicly, for example, that Georgia will be a member.

That was stated twice by the alliance and remains our position, and we believe that all societies should have the right, all countries based on the will of their people, to choose their alliances, their friendships and the organizations that they wish to join. So that is just a basic set of principles.

But that is something that each country should be free to decide for itself. That is the most important principle.

Chairman ROYCE. We go to Mr. Mike McCaul of Texas.

Mr. MCCAUL. Thank you, Mr. Chairman.

Mr. Rubin, I recently went to Russia and I got the sense that Mr. Putin is sort of going back to a Cold War mentality. This is more of a philosophical question.

Do you believe that Russia is intent on reconstituting its empire?

Mr. RUBIN. I think, as I said earlier, I don't really want to speculate about why Russia is doing what it is doing because, honestly, we don't know and I think what we have to judge is simply what is Russia doing.

And what we see Russia doing is what has caused so much concern and that is intervention on the territory of another sovereign state through military force and other coercive means.

Mr. MCCAUL. Well, which—and my time is limited—which they have done prior. I think we learned from history they invaded Georgia and then they continued to occupy Georgia. I think that is very instructive as to the Ukraine experience today.

In fact, Crimea just voted to join Russia. It was announced today and I am concerned that the same thing that happened in Russia will now happen in—that happened in Georgia will happen in Ukraine and I don't know if these sanctions will stop that.

That is my biggest concern. When one nation invades the sovereignty of another we usually—definitions are important—we usually define that as an act of war. Does this administration believe that the Russian invasion of Ukraine is an act of war?

Mr. RUBIN. Well, Congressman, we have said very clearly that we know what we have seen, which is military aggression, intervention in the affairs of a sovereign country—a violation of legal commitments, violation of international law.

That is what we see. That is what we are calling it. I am not an international lawyer so I wouldn't want to get into the terminology but I think it is pretty clear what we are seeing.

It is clear also that Russia continues to occupy territory of the Republic of Georgia. That is something we have been very clear in condemning and it is also clear that their commitments that all countries have to each other to settle their disputes peacefully and that is certainly not what we are seeing here. So I——

Mr. McCaul. Well, I do think we should call it what it is. I think you said it is very clear it is a violation of international law. I believe it is also very clear that this is an act of war against another nation.

When we look at the NATO, I think—I think Mr. Putin feels very threatened by the European Union and NATO. Poland called for an emergency meeting of NATO to discuss its concerns about this Russian aggression. What are we doing to ensure that Poland and our other NATO allies are protected?

Mr. Rubin. Well, one of the things we are doing is increasing our aviation detachment deployment. We are also working to ensure that the Baltic states have the support they need to defend their territory and that is why we have increased our commitments to the Baltic air policing mission with additional planes and refueling, and we are working in Brussels at NATO to address any other concerns that the allies have.

As I said, we take these obligations extremely seriously and we will do our utmost to ensure that the alliance stands together.

Mr. McCaul. Thank you. Thank you, Mr. Chairman.

Chairman Royce. If I can make a quick announcement here before we go Karen Bass of Los Angeles, our strategy will be to recess. I think our witnesses know how Congress operates.

We have got amendments up on the floor to the energy bill. There is about six of these amendments, 2-minute votes. So we will recess until we get to the recommittal debate and that will give us time to come back and finish some of the questioning.

And with that, let us turn to Karen Bass.

Ms. Bass. Thank you, Mr. Chair.

I believe my question is brief and it is for Mr. Singh. Mr. Singh, on Page 3 of your testimony you talk about the IMF and what is needed as an economic adjustment program that eliminates unsustainable economic imbalances and poorly-targeted government subsidies.

I was wondering if you could be more specific as to what those subsidies are, what needs to be changed. And then also is the IMF support contingent on that?

Mr. Singh. Thank you, Congresswoman.

So that is precisely how the IMF works. Its assistance is contingent upon economic reforms being met and these reforms are good for Ukraine and the three core forms that I referenced, number one, there has been an unsustainable build-up in fiscal spending over the years in Ukraine. That needs to be addressed.

Number two, there are truly massive energy subsidies that have been a part that have played——

Ms. BASS. Subsidies to companies or subsidies to the population?

Mr. SINGH. To the population—to tariffs that are paid for heating and gas and so forth. And that has led to consumption of energy that is among the highest in the region.

Ms. BASS. Would you be concerned that some of the reforms might cause problems, dissent if subsidies are cut off? You know what I mean?

Mr. SINGH. So that is why our notion on the loan guarantee is to try to direct the proceeds of that issuance—it is a bond issuance that we have in mind—and direct that toward the more vulnerable segments of the Ukrainian society so that those reforms are easier to implement and that they don't fall on those who can least afford to bear them.

And then the third piece, apart from moving on the energy subsidy problem, which I mentioned has led to over consumption and reliance on Russian gas, I should say, is on their exchange rate.

It is overvalued. It has caused them to have a real problem in terms of exports. It has made their economy uncompetitive.

One last thing is I should say it is very good news in terms of the political will that we are observing on the ground that we are already seeing some movement on these reforms. The currency in Ukraine has weakened quite a bit and become much more flexible.

It is becoming much more driven by market forces. That is a condition of the IMF and the leadership of Ukraine has shown a willingness already to move in that direction. That is a very positive sign.

Ms. BASS. Do you think—I know that elections are supposedly scheduled for May. Do you think there is the leadership there with the current person that is in power just run for election? And that is to anybody. And then thank you, Mr. Chair.

Mr. RUBIN. Congresswoman, the elections have been set for May for the Presidential elections in Ukraine. The candidates have not yet been formally announced nor has anyone formally submitted their candidacies. So we are not sure.

But the current Prime Minister had indicated he would not be a candidate and would just be running the interim government. We will have to see what develops but we do believe it is absolutely critical that there be a fully free, fair election in Ukraine to choose its new President.

Chairman ROYCE. Okay. We are going to go to Mr. Bill Keating of Massachusetts. Would you like to have the last question before we recess?

Mr. KEATING. Thank you, Mr. Chairman. A couple of quick questions.

Number one, NATO Secretary-General Rasmussen has said the alliance plans to intensify its cooperation with Ukraine. Could you give us a more detailed description in terms of NATO's plans and if the Ukrainian Government were to request a membership action plan would the administration consider that, possibly support it? That is question number one.

And the other one simply deals with IMF quota reform. Will that improve the flexibility and to make sure that our dollars and IMF funds are more effectively used and we don't have squandered money—you know, that important taxpayer money from the U.S.

and money from our European allies will that provide more ability to maximize the use of that?

So those are the two questions. Mr. Singh can take the second. I don't know, Mr. Rubin, if you want to take the first.

Mr. RUBIN. Certainly, Congressman. Thank you.

On the question of Ukraine NATO cooperation, Ukraine has been a member of NATO's partnership for peace for two decades and we have a very extensive positive experience working together with Ukraine on training, on improving the readiness, on all sorts of questions that relate to building a modern military—civilian military control and that is something that we certainly hope to continue.

And the Ukraine has admission to NATO. We have regular meetings at the NATO Ukraine council in which that can be discussed and as a matter of fact we just held a session in light of the current events at Ukraine's request.

So we have a very strong partnership through the Partnership for Peace, through the NATO Ukraine council and we do want to continue to develop that with the new government and, in the future, with the new President.

Mr. KEATING. Specifically with the membership action plan, I can't see—in the very near future I can see the need to address this issue, frankly, because our options are limited now and if Ukraine is interested and wants us to pursue this will we entertain those discussions? Will we be supportive?

Mr. RUBIN. Well, Congressman, we have said from the beginning that countries need to be free to choose their memberships, their alliances, their commitments to other countries, that this is basic principle of sovereignty, and therefore as a matter of basic principle NATO is an open alliance.

I think in terms of what the people of Ukraine want, what the Government of Ukraine wants it will be up to them to decide and we will be very interested in having that conversation based on what they tell us.

Mr. KEATING. Okay. On IMF quota reform.

Mr. SINGH. Yes. Congressman, the answer is absolutely. This IMF quota reform would not require a single extra dollar of U.S. financing to the IMF but it would preserve our lead role as the world's preeminent responder, the first responder to financial crisis.

It preserves our voice and our influence at the institution that will be at the very center of the assistance in Ukraine.

And by the way, it also increases the IMF's flexibility to respond to the situation on the ground in the event of the need for a bridge financing to a larger package, which should be a slam dunk.

Mr. KEATING. Okay. Thank you.

Chairman ROYCE. Mr. Deutch, you have a minute, if it is all right.

Mr. DEUTCH. Thank you, Mr. Chairman.

I just have—I want to focus the discussion a different way. In addition to targeting individuals responsible for undermining the democratic process and threatening the territorial integrity of Ukraine, are you considering additional robust sanctions that would have a more significant impact on the Russian regime?

For example, will you look to impose sanctions—Mr. Singh, this is my question to you—will you look to impose sanctions that have been discussed previously for those providing the funding and equipment necessary for the Syrian regime to kill and terrorize its own people?

That, it seems to me, is a way to really strike at Russia in a way that is significant and appropriate.

Mr. SINGH. Congressman, let me just say we have not listed specific individuals or entities today but this is a—this is broad authority that we will use as appropriate, given the situation on the ground.

Mr. DEUTCH. Is it appropriate—is it appropriate to impose sanctions on those individuals who—in Russia who are assisting the Assad regime in slaughtering its own people?

Mr. SINGH. Well, Congressman, I can only say that this specific tool is designed to allow us to sanction those who are most directly involved in destabilizing Ukraine including the military intervention in Crimea.

But it does not preclude further steps to be taken if the situation escalates. I can't comment on your specific question on Syria, unfortunately.

Mr. DEUTCH. So there is—so it does not provide the opportunity. Would you support—do you understand the opportunity though to impose sanctions in a significant way that would impact the Russian regime and the decisions they make by going after those who are responsible for aiding Assad? That is the question you can't answer.

Mr. SINGH. I will have to come back to you with a full response.

Mr. DEUTCH. I appreciate it.

Chairman ROYCE. We stand in recess.

[Recess.]

Chairman ROYCE. Going to go to Mr. Cicilline of Rhode Island.

Mr. CICILLINE. Thank you, Mr. Chairman. I thank you for convening this hearing. Thank you to our witnesses.

I think we all understand the urgency of the moment and the necessity of joining our international—joining an international response to the clear act of Russian aggression, and I presume that many standard review or assessment procedures are likely to be expedited or maybe even waived.

So I would like to just ask you to speak to the sort of long-term obligations of the United States that we are contemplating.

Typically, the United States requires that U.S. credits in volatile countries are administered by an independent facility, administered under U.S. supervision. Will that be the case here? Who will administer Ukraine's payment of interest on the bonds and repayment of principal?

Will the U.S. have effective oversight? How will that occur and what do you assess the prospects for successful repayment and what happens if that does not occur?

And, finally, in addition to the loan guarantee what other sorts of aid is the administration considering for the Ukraine? I assume, Mr. Singh, you would be the best to begin.

Mr. SINGH. Thank you, Congressman.

The way the loan guarantee works is that the U.S. Government guarantees the repayment of the principal and interest on a bond that would be issued by the Ukraine Government.

Okay. So the cost to U.S., the way that it is calculated, is that there is an assessment of the possibility that the Ukraine Government cannot repay the interest in principal, in which case the U.S. Government would be responsible, and that is how it is designed.

Now, the way we can mitigate that risk is twofold. One is that we make the loan guarantee conditional upon the existence of an IMF program, which has strong conditionality and increases the probability of repayment, and, number two, we can use the proceeds from the loan guarantee to lessen the impact of those reforms on the most vulnerable segments of the Ukrainian society and therefore that makes reform implementation—the success of it more likely.

Mr. CICILLINE. And in addition to the loan guarantees, what other aid is the administration considering and what other things can we do to support that?

Ms. ALEXANDER. Thank you for your question, Congressman.

I think the reality is we have had a bilateral support program with Ukraine since 1992 and we have spent a lot of money and we have worked with the government and we have worked with civil society very effectively.

As we look at the Fiscal Year 2015 request that we just made, obviously, that was drawn up, as well as the 2014 request, before we knew what the actual needs were going to be.

So as my colleague was talking about what the IMF team is looking at, USAID in particular will go in and look at the various elements of technical assistance needed to support that, whether it is through banking supervision, whether it is through energy, subsidies, as we were talking about.

But most importantly and immediate, I think we have the elections in front of us and those are something that I think is going to provide a lot of emphasis for the Ukranian people to recognize their true ambitions and where they want to go. And so we want to make sure those are as free, fair and transparent as possible.

Mr. CICILLINE. Thank you very much. I yield back, Mr. Chairman.

Chairman ROYCE. Thank you. Mr. Kennedy of Massachusetts.

Mr. KENNEDY. Thank you, Mr. Chairman. Thank you to the witnesses and I appreciate your testimony earlier. Sorry for the brief break.

Mr. Singh, I wanted to build off a little bit of what one of my colleagues said earlier. Russia has threatened to not use the dollar as the reserve currency. They also have threatened to not pay back some outstanding loans to the U.S. and other European nations.

Are you, again, at all concerned about that or can you assess the validity of that threat—what the economic outcome of that might be?

Mr. SINGH. Congressman, thank you for your question.

I don't think it would be prudent for me to speculate about the various scenarios that could unfold. What I would say again, though, is that Russia does not get to decide whether the U.S. dollar is a reserve currency and that we control our destiny in that regard.

Mr. KENNEDY. And I appreciate that, sir. But with regards to outstanding loans or can you just give me some idea as to the volume of—loans outstanding that they have, if that is a threat? Are we talking about single billions, tens of billions, what kind of order of magnitude where we are at?

Mr. SINGH. We have some initial data on the amount of claims that reside in the U.S. financial system to Russia. Our exposure is somewhat lower than that of Europe, and as it relates to our system in particular it is well under 1 percent.

Mr. KENNEDY. Thank you. And then, perhaps Mr. Rubin or for any of you, I understand from some of the materials that were provided this morning the IMF is currently doing an assessment of the Ukrainian economy at this point.

There has been some issues with transparency, some issues with the full disclosure of the true state of that economy. I think the figures that I have seen at least somewhere between $20 billion and $35 billion over the course of the next year or so.

How long until that full assessment is done and do you—with any degree of certainty are you confident that that figure in there, again, is accurate or is there a potential for what is needed to actually shore up the finances in Ukraine to be quite a bit larger?

Mr. RUBIN. Congressman, thank you for your question.

On the actual figures, I will defer to Mr. Singh. But let me just say that we have been saying now for years that Ukraine needed to address the very serious deficiencies, not just in its economic policy making, but in the entire way its economy was structured.

And we have said all along that the way to do that was to engage in a serious dialogue with the International Monetary Fund, bring in the people who know how to do these assessments and then have a serious negotiation. The previous government did not do that and as a result did not get the help and the advice that it needed.

We are very encouraged by this current interim government's readiness to engage—to engage with the fund, to welcome the advice and to begin making the difficult reforms.

We believe that the package that includes IMF support, that includes IMF quota reform, which we do believe is critical to getting us to be able to have the kind of IMF support to Ukraine and other countries that find themselves in this kind of situation, is a critical part of that package.

And then the bilateral assistance that we are committed to providing together with an IMF package that the European Union has now committed to providing can get Ukraine through this very difficult period but also launch it on a healthy path back toward prosperity and economic stability.

And let me just ask if Mr. Singh had anything to add.

Mr. SINGH. Sure. I will just say that there are a wide range of market estimates out there in terms of Ukraine's financing needs. I don't want to speculate without having the facts.

That is why the IMF is there, as you suggested. They are going to provide that transparency in terms of the financing needs of Ukraine.

I will say that in their estimate of what Ukraine needs much of that is going to depend on the willingness of the Ukranian authorities to undertake the needed reforms and every indication that we have is that they are willing to make the hard decisions.

So I should just add that the IMF and the international community have more than enough resources to meet Ukraine's needs so long as it is willing to make the commitments to reform.

Mr. KENNEDY. And any idea—if I can, Mr. Chairman—just any idea when we will see that report from the IMF? Is that weeks away, days away?

Mr. SINGH. It really depends on the speed with which the relevant data can be handed over and analyzed. It doesn't need to take a long time.

Mr. KENNEDY. Thank you, sir. I appreciate that. Thank you for your time.

Chairman ROYCE. Thank you, Mr. Kennedy. I appreciate it.

Let me ask a question just about the brutality against reporters there—this is one of the concerns I have about the ability to get the free flow of information out around the Ukraine.

We had both Radio Free Europe, Radio Liberty and the Voice of America targeted by security forces there, pro-Yanukovych security forces. We had two Radio Free Europe reporters who were badly beaten and then detained in January.

A prominent journalist and contributor was forced to leave the Ukraine due to death threats in mid-January, and in VOA we had a Ukrainian Service TV reporter who faced repeated intimidation following his coverage of the auto Maidan motorcade protest.

So in the run-up to the next elections in the Ukraine, it seems to me that uncensored information, sort of a surrogate radio to give real-time information about what's actually happening on the ground and to discredit misinformation, is going to be very important.

What steps are being taken to increase messaging to the Ukrainian people and, specifically, one of my concerns is how do you focus that, target that to eastern Ukraine and maybe people in Crimea to make sure that they have got the real case of what is going on?

Ms. ALEXANDER. Thank you, Chairman.

We have been working very effectively with the public diplomacy arm of the Embassy to do exactly that. As you saw, the White House fact sheet yesterday came out about the top 10 myths that are being portrayed out there.

The independent media has been a really bright spot that we have seen throughout Ukraine over the years. Just today, the Ukrainian Crisis Media Center was stood up by Ukrainian activists themselves and these are things that we honestly don't have to financially support because they are doing it themselves.

However, we are trying to give a bit of a bully pulpit and try to amplify the messages that they are putting out. I think you are right.

In the lead-up to the election that will be one of the most important elements is to make sure that this information is out there, and we have been training journalists and we have been working effectively with a lot of burgeoning stations that really have been trying to get the message out.

Chairman ROYCE. I do think, and I have talked to Croatian journalists and others, years ago I tried to restart Radio Free Yugoslavia. By the way, we never had that.

That was the one country we never broadcast in during the Cold War and I have had a number of reporters there tell me that the—you know, you saw the way the Czech Republic and Slovakia handled this without any loss of life.

They told me if there had been a surrogate radio like we had with RFE broadcasting into the country it would have been possible with hate radio for each of these ethnic groups to whip up the types of hatreds that were created.

And that is why I think at the end of the day, having this kind of capability going in before the election while at the same time reassuring Russian-speaking Ukrainians, you know, that the Ukranian Government is going to respect all languages, but I think these broadcasts have to be not just in Ukrainian but in Russian.

I am going to follow up with you on that. But let me just say at this moment we are going to have to adjourn in order to get to the floor for the final vote.

Thank you very much for your testimony here today.

[Whereupon, at 11:01 a.m., the committee was adjourned.]

# APPENDIX

—————

## MATERIAL SUBMITTED FOR THE RECORD

**FULL COMMITTEE HEARING NOTICE**
**COMMITTEE ON FOREIGN AFFAIRS**
U.S. HOUSE OF REPRESENTATIVES
WASHINGTON, DC 20515-6128

**Edward R. Royce (R-CA), Chairman**

March 6, 2014

**TO:    MEMBERS OF THE COMMITTEE ON FOREIGN AFFAIRS**

You are respectfully requested to attend an OPEN hearing of the Committee on Foreign Affairs, to be held in Room 2172 of the Rayburn House Office Building (and available live on the Committee website at http://www.ForeignAffairs.house.gov):

**DATE:**          Thursday, March 6, 2014

**TIME:**          9:00 a.m.

**SUBJECT:**       U.S. Foreign Policy Toward Ukraine

**WITNESSES:**     Mr. Eric Rubin
                   Deputy Assistant Secretary
                   Bureau of European and Eurasian Affairs
                   U.S. Department of State

                   The Honorable Paige Alexander
                   Assistant Administrator
                   Bureau for Europe and Eurasia
                   U.S. Agency for International Development

                   Mr. Daleep Singh
                   Deputy Assistant Secretary for Europe and Eurasia
                   U.S. Department of the Treasury

**By Direction of the Chairman**

*The Committee on Foreign Affairs seeks to make its facilities accessible to persons with disabilities. If you are in need of special accommodations, please call 202/225-5021 at least four business days in advance of the event, whenever practicable. Questions with regard to special accommodations in general (including availability of Committee materials in alternative formats and assistive listening devices) may be directed to the Committee.*

# COMMITTEE ON FOREIGN AFFAIRS
MINUTES OF FULL COMMITTEE HEARING

Day __*Thursday*__ Date __*03/06/14*__ Room __*2172*__

Starting Time __*9:05 A.M.*__ Ending Time __*11:01 A.M.*__

Recesses __*1*__ (__*10:11*__ to __*10:50*__) (___to___) (___to___) (___to___) (___to___) (___to___)

**Presiding Member(s)**

*Rep. Edward R. Royce, Chairman*

*Check all of the following that apply:*

Open Session ☑                     Electronically Recorded (taped) ☑
Executive (closed) Session ☐       Stenographic Record ☑
Televised ☑

**TITLE OF HEARING:**

*U.S Foreign Policy Toward Ukraine*

**COMMITTEE MEMBERS PRESENT:**

*See Attendance Sheet.*

**NON-COMMITTEE MEMBERS PRESENT:**

*None.*

**HEARING WITNESSES: Same as meeting notice attached?** Yes ☑ No ☐
*(If "no", please list below and include title, agency, department, or organization.)*

**STATEMENTS FOR THE RECORD:** *(List any statements submitted for the record.)*

*IFR - Royce*
*IFR- Kennedy*

**TIME SCHEDULED TO RECONVENE** _____
or
**TIME ADJOURNED** *11:01 A.M.*

Jean Marter, Director of Committee Operations

# HOUSE COMMITTEE ON FOREIGN AFFAIRS
*FULL COMMITTEE HEARING*

| PRESENT | MEMBER |
|---|---|
| X | Edward R. Royce, CA |
| X | Christopher H. Smith, NJ |
| X | Ileana Ros-Lehtinen, FL |
| X | Dana Rohrabacher, CA |
| X | Steve Chabot, OH |
|  | Joe Wilson, SC |
| X | Michael T. McCaul, TX |
| X | Ted Poe, TX |
| X | Matt Salmon, AZ |
|  | Tom Marino, PA |
| X | Jeff Duncan, SC |
| X | Adam Kinzinger, IL |
| X | Mo Brooks, AL |
| X | Tom Cotton, AR |
| X | Paul Cook, CA |
| X | George Holding, NC |
| X | Randy K. Weber, Sr., TX |
| X | Scott Perry, PA |
|  | Steve Stockman, TX |
| X | Ron DeSantis, FL |
| X | Doug Collins, GA |
| X | Mark Meadows, NC |
| X | Ted S. Yoho, FL |
| X | Luke Messer, IN |

| PRESENT | MEMBER |
|---|---|
| X | Eliot L. Engel, NY |
|  | Eni F.H. Faleomavaega, AS |
| X | Brad Sherman, CA |
| X | Gregory W. Meeks, NY |
| X | Albio Sires, NJ |
|  | Gerald E. Connolly, VA |
| X | Theodore E. Deutch, FL |
| X | Brian Higgins, NY |
| X | Karen Bass, CA |
| X | William Keating, MA |
| X | David Cicilline, RI |
|  | Alan Grayson, FL |
|  | Juan Vargas, CA |
|  | Bradley S. Schneider, IL |
| X | Joseph P. Kennedy III, MA |
| X | Ami Bera, CA |
| X | Alan S. Lowenthal, CA |
| X | Grace Meng, NY |
| X | Lois Frankel, FL |
| X | Tulsi Gabbard, HI |
| X | Joaquin Castro, TX |

47

ПОСОЛЬСТВО УКРАЇНИ
У СПОЛУЧЕНИХ ШТАТАХ
АМЕРИКИ

EMBASSY OF UKRAINE
TO THE UNITED STATES OF
AMERICA

3350 M Street N.W., Washington, D.C. 20007
Tel.: (202) 349-2920, Fax.: (202) 333-0817
E-mail: emb_us@mfa.gov.ua, www.mfa.gov.ua/usa

Dear Members of Congress:

I would like to begin by thanking the United States of America, and specifically the U.S. Congress, for the unwavering support of Ukraine at these challenging times.

For the past couple of months Ukraine has been in the world's headlines.

The whole world saw the determination of hundreds of thousands of Ukrainians who took to the streets to stand for a better life, for freedom, democracy and end of blatant corruption that stifled our country for far too long.

Yet the Yanukovych regime tried to silence the protesters with guns. Peaceful and unarmed demonstrators were met by special forces with snipers, who shot dead almost a hundred people and wounded hundreds more.

In an attempt to prevent further bloodshed and resolve the crisis, on February 21, 2014 leaders of the opposition Vitalii Klychko, Oleh Tyahnybok and Arsenii Yatsenyuk on one side and Viktor Yanukovych on the other signed an Agreement that had been negotiated with the help of foreign ministers of Poland, Germany and France. Russia's special envoy, Vladimir Lukin, was present but refused to sign it (therefore, the suggestion by the Russian side that the opposition failed to implement the Agreement is groundless).

The Agreement called for an end of violence, restoration of the Ukrainian Constitution of 2004 and early presidential elections.

However, on February 22, 2014 Viktor Yanukovych fled the capital and de facto removed himself from his constitutional authority.

Therefore, on February 22, 2014 the Verkhovna Rada of Ukraine, which was the only legitimate authority in Ukraine at the time, given the resignation of the Government and the President's self-removal from exercising his functions, and restored the 2004 Constitution (approved by 386 votes out of 450), recognized that Viktor Yanukovych removed himself from his constitutional duties through unconstitutional means by 386 votes, including 140 votes from the pro-Yanukovych Party of Regions and set the early elections of the President of Ukraine on May 25, 2014 (328 votes).

According to Article 112 of the Constitution of Ukraine of 2004 in case of early termination of powers of the President of Ukraine the functions of the President of Ukraine shall be carried out by the Speaker of the Parliament until a new President is elected and inaugurated, the only legitimate supreme authority in Ukraine is the Verkhovna Rada of Ukraine. The Rada elected new Speaker, Mr. Oleksandr Turchynov (by 288 votes), who acts as the President of Ukraine until the elections, and appointed Mr. Yatseniuk as the Prime Minister (by 371 votes). These actions were made in full compliance with Ukrainian laws.

However, Russia did not recognize these changes and considers Viktor Yanukovych a legitimate President.

Producing a piece of paper purporting to be Mr. Yanukovych's letter asking Mr. Putin to send Russian troops to Ukraine, the Federation Council of Russia, upon Mr. Putin's request, approved such decision.

Mr. Yanukovych is no longer the President of Ukraine, particularly after his escape from Kyiv on February 22, 2014. Therefore, none of his statements have any significance under either Ukrainian or international law.

But in any way, even if the legitimate President of Ukraine called upon a foreign country to intervene with its armed forces in Ukraine, such a statement would also be worth nothing, because under the Constitution of Ukraine (Art. 85) only the Verhovna Rada of Ukraine can approve decisions on admitting units of armed forces of other states to the territory of Ukraine. The Rada clearly stated that it had not made any such decisions.

Seeing that Ukraine is determined to pursue its European course, Russia, under the completely trumped up pretext invaded Crimea with its armed forces.

The Russian forces are seeking to establish complete control over Ukraine's military facilities in Crimea, trying to block and disarm Ukrainian military garrisons and border guard bases, blocking airports and ships. The Russian troops and armored vehicles are moving uncontrollably around Crimea, numerous Russian military planes and helicopters violated Ukrainian airspace.

By countless provocations, Russian military is seeking to instigate an armed conflict and replicate in Ukraine the Abkhazia and South Ossetia scenario. However, Ukrainian servicemen act with utmost restraint and don't react to such provocations, but there's a threat that Russia may engineer provocations against its own troops, and blame them on Ukraine.

There is also an ongoing accumulation of military equipment on the Russian territory in close proximity to the border of Ukraine in the Kharkiv, Luhansk, Donetsk and Chernihiv oblasts. These actions may indicate preparations of the Russian side for possible intervention into the Ukrainian territory across the land border.

The military intervention is accompanied by a huge outburst of fabrications. I can assure you that Russian-speaking citizens of Ukraine enjoy the same rights and freedoms as other citizens of my country. Nobody has ever forbidden, forbids or will forbid the use of the Russian language, as the Russian propaganda tries to demonstrate. As of today there is no proof of any violations of Russian minority rights in Ukraine; there were no appeals to the relevant Ukrainian authorities neither from those allegedly affected nor from Russia's officials. In accordance with the Memorandum of Understanding between the Parliamentary Commissioner on Human Rights of Ukraine and the Ombudsman of the Russian Federation in case of such appeals to the Russian side they are transferred to the Ukrainian Ombudsman.

The actions by the Russian Federation constitute an act of aggression against the state of Ukraine. Russian Federation brutally violated the basic principles of Charter of the United Nations obliging all member states to refrain from the threat or use of force against the territorial integrity or political independence of any state.

49

Ukraine in the strongest possible terms protested such actions, but Russia officially rejected Ukrainian proposal to hold immediate bilateral consultations (under Article 7 of the Treaty on Friendship, Cooperation and Partnership between Ukraine and the Russian Federation of 1997).

Russia's actions pose a serious threat not only to the sovereignty and territorial integrity of Ukraine, but also to peace and stability in the whole region. Moreover, Russia's actions provoke a disbalance in the international security system and can lead to violations of the regime of international nuclear non-proliferation on a global scale.

When in 1994, Ukraine became a party to Non-Proliferation Treaty and voluntarily surrendered the third largest nuclear arsenal in the world it did so exclusively under certain conditions. These conditions envisaged granting security assurances to Ukraine by the 5 nuclear states. On December 5, 1994, the United States, the Russian Federation and the United Kingdom signed the Budapest Memorandum on Security Assurances to Ukraine. The French Republic and the People's Republic of China supported the Memorandum by signing separate declarations.

Ukraine has thoroughly implemented its commitments under the Non-Proliferation Treaty, and has taken and fulfilled additional obligations by getting rid of all its stockpiles of highly enriched uranium.

Today we witness the situation when the Russian Federation attempts to undermine the NPT regime not only by violating the Budapest Memorandum, but also by violating the Non-Proliferation Treaty, which clearly states in its Preamble that "States must refrain in their international relations from the threat or use of force against the territorial integrity or political independence of any State, or in any other manner".

Non-adherence by one Guarantor State – the Russian Federation – to its commitments under the Budapest Memorandum by the military invasion in Ukraine creates a situation when the threshold states may consider international legal instruments insufficient to ensure security, territorial integrity and inviolability of their borders.

We rely on the commitments contained in the Budapest Memorandum of 1994 and the Charter on a Distinctive Partnership between NATO in Ukraine, as well as the U.S.-Ukraine Charter on Strategic Partnership and other bilateral documents. We need help from the guarantor states, the UN, NATO, the OSCE, the European Union, all civilized nations to protect our sovereignty and territorial integrity by all available means and to prevent a war which would shatter peace in Europe and will have grave and irrevocable consequences for peace and security on a global scale.

The aggression must be stopped, and we rely on the strong and unified position of the global community.

Military units deployed from Russia must leave the territory of Ukraine immediately, and those belonging to the Russian Black Sea Fleet must return to their barracks. Armed gangs that came from Russia must also immediately leave Ukraine.

Crimea is an inalienable part of Ukraine, with citizens of all ethnic backgrounds.

All issues should be resolved through negotiations. There is no alternative to a peaceful and diplomatic solution of the crisis. We hope that wisdom will prevail. We need America's help, and we count on it.

Sincerely yours,

Olexandr Motsyk
Ambassador of Ukraine to the United States

**Statement for the Record**
*Submitted by the Honorable Joe Kennedy*

Thank you Chairman Royce and Ranking Member Engel for calling this hearing today and for inviting the witnesses to testify on the current situation in Ukraine. I ask unanimous consent to submit the following Council on Foreign Relations article to the record.

# An Energy Weapon vs. Russia?

http://blogs.cfr.org/levi/2014/03/05/an-energy-weapon-vs-russia/?cid=nlc-public-the_world_this_week-link9-20140307&sp_mid=45296923&sp_rid=am9lLmtlbm5lZHlAZ21haWwuY29tS0

by Michael Levi
March 5, 2014

As the standoff between Russia and Ukraine drags on, there are increasing calls to use U.S. oil and gas exports to weaken Vladimir Putin's hand. There's something to this, but it's likely to be a lot less powerful than most pundits seem to think.

Europe imports about thirty percent of its natural gas from Russia. Russia could, in principle, cut off some or all of that supply. That prospect presumably makes European leaders less willing to take strong positions against Russia in its confrontation with Ukraine. People have argued that boosting U.S. natural gas export capacity (or, more precisely, changing policy to make that more likely in the future) could do two things. First, in the current crisis, it could deter Putin from using the gas weapon, lest he encourage Europeans to make concerted efforts to shift their long-term gas procurement to the United States when that becomes possible in a few years. Second, in future crises, it could blunt the Russian gas weapon, since U.S. exports would be available to fill in for Russian supplies.

(You might have noticed that I haven't said anything about oil. That's because the idea that U.S. oil exports would give Europe some sort of special buffer is silly. The world oil market is pretty flexible, and U.S. exports would be a drop in an already large sea. To the extent that Europe is constrained in its ability to switch oil sources quickly, that's because of infrastructure, something U.S. exports wouldn't change.)

There are two essential things to keep in mind when thinking through the claims about natural gas exports.

First, decisions about whom to export to and import from are made by commercial entities, not by governments. When a U.S. analyst says, "we should tell Europe we'll sell them our gas", the first response should be, "who's 'we'"? (The second response should be, "who's Europe?") The U.S. government doesn't get to sell gas to anyone; it can create a framework in which commercial entities can sell gas, but after that, it's up to those businesses to decide where the gas goes. Similarly, "Europe" doesn't buy gas – all sorts of European companies do, within European and national regulatory frameworks.

Second, surging natural gas into Europe to respond to a crisis requires that there be infrastructure in place that can accommodate that surge. In the case we're talking about here, that means having a bunch of unused (or partly used) European natural gas import terminals that can suddenly absorb newly arrived U.S. supplies. And remember – back to the first point – these terminals will be built by private players.

So what does this all mean for the big strategic claims?

It is difficult to see how U.S. exports will substantially erode the long-run share of Russian gas in Europe. It is far more profitable for buyers of U.S. natural gas to ship it to Asia – where prices are far higher – than to Europe. (The exception is if European companies are willing to pay a hefty premium to get their gas from the United States – but remember, these are commercial entities, which makes it very difficult for them to do that.) There is, of course, a knock on effect from that, since if U.S. gas frees up other supplies that were destined for Asia, those supplies can potentially move into Europe instead. But Russia remains a relatively low-cost supplier into Europe, and can trim its prices to keep its market share. Moreover, unlike European gas companies, the big Russian players have much tighter ties with the state. If Moscow wants them to keep their share in the European market for strategic reasons, it may be able to make them do that. Russia would lose money – an important piece of geopolitical harm – but its leverage wouldn't be slashed.

What about supplying gas to Europe in a crisis? Here the basic constraint is infrastructure. Gas demand is seasonal, so during some parts of the year, there may be underutilized LNG import terminals. [UPDATE 3/6: Moreover, with a weak European economy, there is currently a lot of unutilized European LNG import capacity year-round; whether that persists indefinitely remains to be seen. Even in the current case, though, Russian imports into Europe greatly exceed spare LNG import capacity.] Were Russia to cut gas supplies to Europe during a crisis, if prices rose high enough, those terminals could be used to surge in some supplies. During other times (notably winter, when gas demand is most acute) the terminals will be fully utilized, making them unavailable to bring in new LNG supplies. The only way around that is to overbuild. This might happen by mistake, but unless European policymakers offer financial incentives, profit-seeking firms won't do it on purpose.

There is one other wrinkle worth thinking about here. The United States is currently able to take a harder line against Russia than Europeans are in part because the U.S. economy is insulated from energy-related turmoil. Were the prospect of surging gas into Europe a real one, we'd be having all sorts of debates here about the economic fallout for the United States from escalation with Russia. [UPDATE 3/6: It's worth distinguishing here between swinging U.S. gas from Asian to European customers, which wouldn't affect the U.S. market, and boosting total U.S. exports, which would.] Ironically, while being more connected to European gas markets might give the United States more tools in a future crisis, it could also deter Washington from aggressively confronting Russia.